Cambridge Elements ≡

Elements in Austrian Economics
edited by
Peter Boettke
George Mason University

JAMES BUCHANAN AND PEACEFUL COOPERATION

From Public Finance to a Theory of Collective Action

Alain Marciano
University of Torino

CAMBRIDGE
UNIVERSITY PRESS

Shaftesbury Road, Cambridge CB2 8EA, United Kingdom

One Liberty Plaza, 20th Floor, New York, NY 10006, USA

477 Williamstown Road, Port Melbourne, VIC 3207, Australia

314–321, 3rd Floor, Plot 3, Splendor Forum, Jasola District Centre,
New Delhi – 110025, India

103 Penang Road, #05–06/07, Visioncrest Commercial, Singapore 238467

Cambridge University Press is part of Cambridge University Press & Assessment,
a department of the University of Cambridge.

We share the University's mission to contribute to society through the pursuit of
education, learning and research at the highest international levels of excellence.

www.cambridge.org
Information on this title: www.cambridge.org/9781009493796

DOI: 10.1017/9781009493826

First published 2024

A catalogue record for this publication is available from the British Library.

ISBN 978-1-009-49379-6 Hardback
ISBN 978-1-009-49377-2 Paperback
ISSN 2399-651X (online)
ISSN 2514-3867 (print)

Cambridge University Press & Assessment has no responsibility for the persistence
or accuracy of URLs for external or third-party internet websites referred to in this
publication and does not guarantee that any content on such websites is, or will
remain, accurate or appropriate.

James Buchanan and Peaceful Cooperation

From Public Finance to a Theory of Collective Action

Elements in Austrian Economics

DOI: 10.1017/9781009493826
First published online: June 2024

Alain Marciano
University of Torino
Author for correspondence: Alain Marciano, alain.marciano@unito.it

Abstract: Buchanan believed that individuals are fundamentally willing to cooperate with others. It was at the center of his works in public finance in the late 1940s and early 1950s, and also crucial to his work in public choice in the 1960s. The purpose of this book is to show which forms this belief took over these two decades or so, and to explain the continuity between these forms. We adopt a historical approach that allows us to recount the story of how Buchanan came to develop a theory of collective action, including his conception of cooperation in small groups, to implement a technical condition about the pricing of public goods he defended early in his career. We describe the different steps Buchanan took, the encounters that influenced him, and the events and challenges that led him to revise his views to make room for this fundamental philosophical conviction.

Keywords: Buchanan, political economy, public choice, history of economic thought, US history

ISBNs: 9781009493796 (HB), 9781009493772 (PB), 9781009493826 (OC)
ISSNs: 2399-651X (online), 2514-3867 (print)

Contents

1. University of Turin (It), Department Economics and Statistics, 2. Distinguished Affiliated Fellow, F. A. Hayek Program for Advanced Study in Philosophy, Politics, and Economics, 3. Karl Mittermaier Centre for Philosophy of Economics, University of Johannesburg.

1 Introduction

James Buchanan emphasized, in his introduction of the *Thomas Jefferson Center for Studies in Political Economy* published in the University of Virginia News Letter in October 1958 (1958c), that the objective of the Center was to "carry on the honorable tradition of 'political economy' – the study of what makes for a 'good society'" (1958c: 5). Which, to Buchanan, meant a "free society" (5). The expansion of individual freedom, not its contraction, had caused the "accelerating improvement in material standards of wellbeing previously undreamed of" (5). This was why Buchanan – along with G. Warren Nutter and Rutledge Vining – created the Jefferson Center, to gather "a community of scholars who wish to preserve a social order based on individual liberty" (5). Buchanan insisted that political economists should "examine philosophical values for consistency among themselves and with the ideal of human freedom" (5). He also noted that political economists "stress the technical economic principles that one must understand in order to assess alternative arrangements for promoting peaceful cooperation and productive specialization among free men" (5).

Defining the goal and purpose of political economy in this way reveals a belief, a strong conviction in Buchanan: Peaceful cooperation does exist. Put in different words, Buchanan believed that the scope for voluntary cooperative (spontaneous) and private action is significantly broader than commonly acknowledged. And complementarily, the scope for government intervention is much reduced compared to what is typically argued. This means that even when markets do not function correctly, especially in the presence of public goods and externalities, individuals can find ways to coordinate their actions and cooperate with others. This was a philosophical conviction Buchanan held, that underpinned his social philosophy – individuals are fundamentally inclined, and willing to cooperate with others. It was at the center of his works in public finance in the late 1940s and early 1950s, and was equally pivotal in his contributions to public choice theory in the 1960s. The purpose of the book is to show which forms this conviction took over these two decades and to explain the continuity between these forms.

Our starting point lies in what Buchanan wrote in the late 1940s and in the early 1950s, which includes the famous paper "The Pure Theory of Government Finance: A Suggested Approach" (1949b). In this work, Buchanan adheres to what is known as the voluntary exchange theory in public finance and to one of its major principles, namely that public goods should be priced as private goods. This implies that individuals should pay a specific, individualized price for the public goods and services they consume. Individualized prices are a condition for a voluntary exchange between the government and citizens/taxpayers. Buchanan tirelessly defended individualized prices, even when most of his colleagues criticized and gave up using them and even when decision-makers refused to envisage using such prices in public policies. One of the major obstacles was the implementation of such prices. In other words, the problem Buchanan had to face was of an institutional nature. To answer the criticism, to find a way to use a principle he had put at the center of his public finance theory, Buchanan had to pay attention to collective action and propose a theory of collective action. This theory is found in *The Calculus of Consent* (1962) as well as many other works written in the early 1960s.

The development of such a theory not only allowed Buchanan to find a mechanism to implement individualized prices – clubs (1965a) – but also to discuss the conditions under which individuals would agree to pay such prices. Clubs were the institution through which individuals could pay for what they consume and, at the same time, guarantees that they do pay for what they consume. In the early-mid 1960s, Buchanan became less certain than before about individuals always willing to pay for public goods or internalize the externalities resulting from their actions. Certain conditions had to be met. It revolved around property rights and numbers. The size of the group in which individuals who decide to produce a public good matters. Individuals do not behave the same way in small groups as in large groups. It is not that they are no longer self-interested, but they understand that pursuing their self-interest requires them to behave strategically and take others into account. This leads individuals to behave ethically.

Thus Buchanan's theory of collective action, including his conception of cooperation in small groups, comes from a technical condition about the pricing of public goods which he defended early in his career. Buchanan's works in public finance are crucial to understanding his works in public choice and his attempt at building a theory of collective action, which comes from a desire to deal with a problem in public finance.

This thesis parallels and complements Richard Wagner's monograph *James M. Buchanan and Liberal Political Economy: A Rational Reconstruction* (2017). This present work, however, emphasizes that "The Pure Theory of

Government Finance" contained only seeds that might have not blossomed, promises that might not have been realized. They only did so because of certain events that took place around Buchanan, that pushed him and led him to pay attention to institutions and to develop a theory of collective action. This work contends that Buchanan became interested in public choice because he was a public finance economist.

What follows is a historical a narrative in which Buchanan's various articles are linked to the question of individualized pricing. We describe the different steps Buchanan made to find a way to accommodate his belief in individualized prices and propose what an alternative history on the origins of Buchanan's theory of collective action. The history reveals that Buchanan kept adjusting his theory to deal with the problems and difficulties raised by other thinkers with whom he disagreed but took seriously – Paul A. Samuelson, John K. Galbraith, or Richard A. Musgrave. He also continued to adjust his theory to include elements he learned from thinkers with whom he agreed – such as Rutledge Vining or Gordon Tullock. Buchanan was a lifelong learner, in constant dialogue with his peers and colleagues.

2 Spillover Effects, the Pricing of Roads, and the Problem of Social Cost

2.1 The Foundations: Exchange, Benefits, and Voluntarism

Buchanan's conviction that markets or, at least, decentralized mechanisms work well is based on his confidence in individuals. Individuals, Buchanan believed, are willing to pay for the goods they consume, whether private or public – and are also ready to pay for the external effects their actions give birth to. This is a belief that Buchanan espoused very early in his career, as illustrated by the adoption of "voluntary exchange theory" in his doctoral dissertation.[1] Buchanan had read (some of) Knut Wicksell, Erik Lindhal, Emil Sax, Adolph Wagner, and the members of the so-called Italian School of Finance, Antonio De Viti de Marco, Maffeo Pantaleoni, and Ugo Mazzola, and based his dissertation (1948) on their works. He cited them again in the important "The Pure Theory of Government Finance" (1949a, 1949b), which is entirely based on the voluntary exchange theory of public finance.

"The fundamental position taken by this theory," Buchanan noted in his dissertation, "is that the individual's financial relations with government are basically analogous to any private economic transaction; they consist of an exchange relationship" (1948: 51–52). Taxes are prices, the prices individuals

---

[1] For a presentation of the origins of voluntary exchange theories, see Johnson (2015).

pay to obtain the goods and services provided by the state. They are, Buchanan wrote, a "return for services rendered" (44). A few pages later, he noted that "taxes or contributions paid are exchanged for services rendered by the political unit" (52), a sentence which appears almost word for word in the article published in 1949: Taxes are the "payment made by individuals out of their economic resources in exchange for services provided" (1949b: 498).

Complementarily, taxes cannot be a "burden" or "net subtractions from social income, never to be returned" (500), as it was assumed by many public finance theorists.[2] To him, it is "impossible to speak of the 'burden of taxation' without considering, at the same time, the benefits from expenditure made out of such taxation" (501). By excluding benefits – that is, by seeing taxes as a burden only – one could not understand why transactions with the government are voluntary: Taxes are paid *because* individuals receive benefits from paying them. Thus, Buchanan adopted a benefit theory of taxation.

And Buchanan did mean *individual* benefits. A certain ambiguity seems to blur his purpose at the beginning. Buchanan discussed the "collective willingness of individuals to purchase" (1949b: 499) public services, and referred to "the collective equalization of benefits and taxes" (502) and to "collective wants" (1948: 52) or "collective desires" (1949b: 505), and even explained that "[i]deally, the fiscal process represents a *quid pro quo* transaction between the government and all individuals collectively considered" (499). Yet, Buchanan adopted an individualistic approach – he was opposed to "organicism" and insisted that the voluntary exchange approach is individualist.[3] To Buchanan, the collectivity was nothing more than the sum of individuals and does not – cannot – exist independently from the individuals. As a consequence, "[i]f benefits from public services accrue to individuals as a group (and this is impossible to deny), it follows that specific benefits are received by particular individuals" (500).

Certainly, these benefits are difficult, to say the least, to evaluate for each individual because they are subjective. And accordingly, Buchanan agreed that

---

[2] Namely by those who adopt an "organismic" approach he identified in public finance (Buchanan 1948, 1949a, 1949b). Buchanan indeed opposed the "two separate and conflicting theories of the State . . . upon which a 'pure' theory of government finance might be constructed" (1949a: 2): the "organismic" and the "individualistic" theories of the state (or government finance). He associated the "organismic" with the current and orthodox approach in government finance. In his first works, Buchanan did not give many names of representatives of the organismic approach. Arthur Pigou was one of them. Musgrave would have qualified (Johnson, 2015: 10).

[3] For instance, he wrote, "The state has no ends other than those of its individual members and is not a separate decision-making unit. State decisions are, in the final analysis, the collective decisions of individuals" (1949b: 498). According to Bernd Hansjürgens (2000), one of the most original and unusual features of Wicksell's analysis was his individualism (2000: 99). Undoubtedly, this appealed to Buchanan.

it will be "extremely difficult, if not impossible" to determine the exact tax each beneficiary would have to pay in proportion "to his gain in subjective utility resulting from the free provision of the service" (1951: 175). Wicksell was also aware of the problem, and had dismissed it. Buchanan insisted, "Wicksell does not rely upon any accurate measurement or even approximation of total consumers' surplus arising from the provision of the particular public service in question" and that "Wicksell is not very concerned about this estimation being too accurate" (176). However, this was not a problem. There was no need to measure these benefits or to evaluate this surplus. What mattered was that such a surplus exists and that the individuals themselves were able to evaluate it:

> [s]ince the total costs of the enterprise must be paid exclusively by those receiving the benefits of the service provided, all that is required is that each beneficiary (or enough of them to pay the general costs) make some estimation of his surplus and be willing to contribute its value equivalent. (177)

Therefore, this aspect of the discussion was secondary. It remained a practical problem, a problem of implementation, that should not be confused with a fundamental problem. The difficulty of evaluating individual benefits is not substantial, but (simply) empirical. What matters is that each individual gains something from paying their taxes. And, from this perspective, there is no doubt that benefits exist. Buchanan thus wrote that the individual's "satisfactions are increased by the government services provided him and theoretically this increase in utility can be reduced to value terms" (1948: 56). Indeed, his defense of benefits, and thus of "voluntary exchange," was not pure speculation but the logical conclusion of a reasoning with no empirical dimension. For Buchanan, the existence of benefits and his belief in an individualist benefit principle were not simply grounded in a philosophical conviction. Their existence was a fact, which could be observed and verified empirically, even if indirectly. The fact that individuals pay taxes or vote for politicians who propose programs that involve public spending and taxes proves that they derive a benefit from paying these taxes. In the absence of benefits, such behaviors became incomprehensible. Wicksell had stressed this point correctly, Buchanan noted (1949b: 500).[4]

---

[4] The difference with Musgrave is striking. As we will see later, Musgrave found voluntary exchange theories in public finance unrealistic because, to him, individuals did not voluntarily pay taxes. They have to be coerced. Buchanan and Musgrave clearly interpreted Wicksell differently. On these differences see Johnson (2005).

The price individuals are ready to pay – and their demand at this price – indicates the upper limit of the price they are willing to pay, exactly as is the case with private goods. Of course, the greater the difference, the larger the individual surplus. And, sometimes – in particular, when they are able to "conceal their true preferences" – certain individuals "will be able to secure the proportionately larger share of the gains to be made by the 'trade'" (1960a, 238). But none of this would be a problem. As long as individuals gain something from the trade – with the government or with other individuals – they voluntarily pay their taxes, pay for the public goods they want to consume, and internalize the external effects their actions generate. To put it differently, the Pareto frontier will be reached.

2.2 Unanimity and Voluntarism

Buchanan then shifted his focus to efficiency. This was not at the heart of his early works (1947, 1948, 1949a, and 1949b). But in 1951, he referred to efficiency, resource allocation, and explained why a Wicksellian scheme, based on exchange and mutual gains from trade, guarantees optimal resource allocation. The reason: Wicksell's theory is "in accordance with the principle of unanimity" (1951: 177).

The article in which Buchanan makes his case was written with a specific aim, to show that Knut Wicksell's theory of voluntary exchange was perfectly relevant to answering most of the questions raised in the debate on the possibility to set price at the marginal cost of production (particularly for public enterprises and enterprises with decreasing costs). Buchanan had begun translating Wicksell's *Finanztheoretische Untersuchungen*, but ran into major difficulties when two articles by Nancy Ruggles (1949a, 1949b) on welfare economics and marginal cost pricing were published. In her analysis, Ruggles referred to Wicksell and, more specifically, to Wicksell's only book to have then been translated into English, his *Lectures of Political Economy* (Wicksell 1934). Ruggles had made a few remarks that did not correspond with how Buchanan understood Wicksell. And she said nothing of Wicksell and marginal cost pricing. This worried Buchanan and piqued his interest. An article he himself described as "the most complete discussion of the history and development of the principle of marginal cost pricing" (1951: 173) was not, however, as complete as it could have been. Nor was Ruggles alone in facing this problem. Her work suffered from the same limitation as the rest of the literature on Wicksell: It "acknowledged" Wicksell's "contribution in formalizing the conditions under which perfect competition tends to maximize economic welfare," noted Buchanan (1951: 173), but made "little reference to his work in specific relation to the problem of pricing for firms with decreasing costs," or rather, made no mention of it at all (1951: 173, fn 4). Buchanan knew Wicksell's contribution on marginal cost pricing because it "appears in the middle of his *FU*" [*Finanztheoretische Untersuchungen*] (1951: 173). He had read the book.

Buchanan certainly found Wicksell's views that it was possible to equate the price with the marginal cost – or even zero, if marginal costs were nonexistent – and then to cover the rest of the costs of production and operation with tax revenues useful for the debate on marginal cost pricing. But what interested him more was that Wicksell's message went far beyond the efficiency of marginal cost pricing. This had already been noticed by Richard Musgrave, who had discussed Wicksell in broader terms. Musgrave had nonetheless dismissed Wicksell's theory of voluntary exchange as "highly unrealistic" (1939, 419; see also 1941, 322) and "of little practical significance" (1939: 220) because it was based on *voluntarism*. Indeed, Musgrave had noted, that "[d]irect compulsion prevails in the legal enforcement of individual tax contributions" (219). It thus made no sense to Musgrave to argue that voluntary transactions took place between the government and the taxpayers. There was a good reason for "the predominantly compulsory nature of the actual revenue-expenditure process" (219): "the absence of a general willingness to comply with the obligation to contribute" (220). Or, to use an anachronistic term that Musgrave did not employ – individuals free ride.

Buchanan did not refer to Musgrave in his 1951 article on marginal cost pricing – but he obviously disagreed with him. That was precisely because of "its essential element of voluntarism" (1951: 178) that Buchanan found Wicksell's analysis of the pricing of goods with decreasing costs relevant. To Wicksell, Buchanan explained, public enterprises should "charg[e] fees equal to the marginal costs of providing the service and making up the deficit by tax revenues" (174). Indeed, Buchanan insisted, "the most advantageous method of operation is always given by the marginal cost principle, with the fixed costs covered by taxation" (176). More precisely, unlike Lerner and Hotelling for whom taxes should be levied on all taxpayers – including nonusers – in a nondiscriminatory way, Wicksell proposed that only users pay the taxes raised to finance the deficit caused by the difference between average and marginal costs. That was consistent with what Buchanan had written earlier – in his dissertation and in his 1949 article on the pure theory of government finance – namely that taxes should be paid by "the individuals who benefit from the proposed enterprise." Wicksell's solution, Buchanan noted, thus "does not require collection of taxes from any one other than the specific beneficiaries" or "[t]he losses must be made up from 'contributions' paid by those benefited" (178).

Wicksell's solution was possible because it was assumed that users would willingly pay taxes because of the benefits they receive from consuming public goods and services. Put differently, the individuals' willingness to pay or to contribute could be explained by the benefits received from the consumption of any good or the use of any service. Wicksell had even suggested that these benefits could be evaluated. For instance, Buchanan (1951: 175) referred to the example Wicksell had used, that a public enterprise would cost 100,000 annually to run but would generate a subjective value of at least 226,000. In that case, the existence of a surplus was obvious and was evidence that the firm should exist. It is the comparison of the total costs with the total *utility*, and not with the total revenues, that Wicksell used as "[t]he criterion for determining whether or not an enterprise should be undertaken" (176).

Since, as mentioned earlier, the question of individual evaluation could be set aside, Wicksell's theory was disarmingly simple to put into practice. This simplicity stemmed from its reliance on individuals and their willingness to pay, eliminating the possibility of free-riding, to use a term that was not then used. This solved the problem of whether or not a public good or service should be provided. Then, there was a question of how to allocate the tax burdens among individuals. Buchanan answered by referring to the solution proposed by Wicksell, which consisted in using the principle of unanimity. Unanimity worked as a necessary condition to be fulfilled when decisions were made about the provision of public goods. In other words, marginal cost pricing could function with a specific voting rule.

Unanimity served two purposes. First, justice. In the words of Wicksell (1896 [1958]: 90), "if justice requires no more, it certainly requires no less. In the final analysis, unanimity and fully voluntary consent in the making of decisions provide the only certain and palpable guarantee against injustice in tax distribution." Unanimity was "a guarantee against action designed to benefit or harm special classes unjustly" (Buchanan 1951: 176), a means to avoid the "tyranny of the majority" (1948: 11) and a means to protect "the working and poorer" (Johnson 2010: 193). Second, efficiency. Buchanan insisted, since "no one is worse off if some allocation of the required tax can be found which is acceptable to everyone," unanimity guaranteed that the "Paretian conditions for optimum welfare" (177) are satisfied without relying on any centralized mechanism.

Thus, the fundamental principles of Buchanan's political economy that were present in the early 1950s are individualized prices for public goods – taxes are prices –, voluntarism and willingness to pay, and unanimity – the tax structure should be determined by asking *all* individuals how much they are ready to contribute. It remained to apply this framework, to test it so to speak. With particular reference to cases in which individual consumption creates external effects, that is when there are public goods. This is what Buchanan did starting in 1952.

2.3 Roads and the Problem of Social Cost

2.3.1 An Important and Topical Question

Transportation infrastructure was already a topic of interest for Buchanan in the early 1940s, when he was still at the University of Tennessee Knoxville, when he was writing his master thesis (see Marciano 2019). He then argued that users should pay for using roads and highways. About ten years later, roads and highways were still important for Buchanan as they were an instrument for the development of the American South, which was crucial to Buchanan (see Marciano 2020). They were also an issue for the USA in general.

By the late 1940s and early 1950s, it was not only necessary to maintain the existing network but also to build new infrastructure, partly because the size of the metropolitan areas had increased dramatically – they accounted for 81 percent of the country's population growth –, as had the rate of motorization – up to 50 percent between 1945 and 1955 – while public transportation was in decline. The amount of money that were required were enormous. Thus, the Joint Economic Committee on "Highways and the Nation's Economy," in cooperation of the Bureau of Public Roads, found that:

> [t]he total cost of correcting the present deficiencies on the highways, roads, and streets of the Nation... at $41,144,630,000. Of this amount, $7,700,000,000 is estimated as the amount needed for city and village streets, and $10,400,000,000 for the correction of deficiencies on the local rural roads. The remaining $23,044,630,320 is the amount needed for the State highway systems and their urban extensions. (1950: 8).

As a consequence, building and maintaining roads had indeed become:

> a major governmental activity by every measure. Expenditures in 1950 approximated $4.25 billion, an all-time high. The total of permanent and temporary employees numbers in the hundreds of thousands. At both state and local levels highways compete with education and welfare for first place in terms of money. (Redfield and Lutz 1952: 127)

Yet, despite this increasing government intervention, the pace at which roads were built or renovated remained too slow. To remedy the problem, government intervention was further increased. In May 1950, the Congress passed a bill that expanded the Federal-aid program and increased the share of the federal government. One month later, the Korea war erupted. Consequently, and rather unsurprisingly, roads became a secondary matter and public spending on road infrastructure was cut down.[5] The problem became worse. Nothing, or almost nothing, happened until two years later when the 1952 Federal-Aid Highway Act authorized $550 million a year for the primary and secondary system plus a token of $25 million for the interstate network of highways. That was better but still far from what had been estimated in 1949. In 1951, it was estimated that "approximately 6.5 billion dollars annually will be required to modernize and maintain the highway system during the next decade . . . to bring the highway system to acceptable standards" (Owen and Dearing 1951: 25). The gap between needs and what was actually done was such that Dick Netzer, an economist at the Federal Reserve Bank of Chicago, spoke of "the crisis in highway finance" (1952: 107).

Building toll roads was one possible solution. There was, in the early 1950s, a "revival of the toll road" (Owen and Dearing 1951: 21). Netzer thus explained that toll roads were interesting because they could be "financed through borrowing without general increases in user tax rates" (1952: 108). But there were drawbacks too. They seemed more costly to build than free roads – "there can be no crossings at grade; the right of way must generally be fenced throughout; etc" (113). Also, they often duplicated existing roads, which suggests that it might be less costly to improve the latter than to build new ones. Then, toll roads could not be used anywhere – for instance in cities. And, finally, the improvements obtained by building toll roads, to the benefit of a few users, could reduce or even remove the incentives to improve the more frequently used free roads. Netzer thus doubted that, despite their success, toll roads could be "the *best* solution to the elements of the critical highway problem" (119, emphasis in original).

Buchanan first wrote a short article devoted to congestion, published on February 5 in the section "Public Opinion-Reader's Views" of the *Tallahassee Democrat*. He claimed that "[t]he excessive congestion is basically a reflection of the fact that the road and street system of the nation are not being operated properly. There are too many cars for the available supply of roads and streets." To solve the problem one could build more highways, but this takes a long time. The alternative was "to make riding on the highways more expensive by

---

[5] As noted in the October 1950 issue of *American Highways*, the magazine of the American Association of State Highway Officials: "Our peacetime economy is built around highway transportation; in war, our very survival depends upon it. And yet, the people have not been made to understand these facts. Why? Where have we failed?" (https://www.fhwa.dot.gov/publications/publicroads/02may/08.cfm).

increasing the prices charged highway users." Indeed, congestion was due to the fact that "the states and municipalities are not charging car owners high enough 'prices' for the use of highway facilities." In a "free enterprise system . . . prices . . . prevent shortages of goods." If the prices of any goods were too low – for instance, "if round steak was priced at 50 c per pound," – "[t]here would be excessive congestion around the meat counters in our grocery store." This is what was happening with highways. Why not use prices to prevent the shortage of highway infrastructure? Since this was what congestion was about – "a shortage of highway facilities at the prevailing price charged for these facilities." This was exactly the reasoning he developed in an article published in the *National Tax Journal*.

2.3.2 The Pricing of Highway Services and the Problem of Social Cost

"The pricing of highway services" (1952) begins with a criticism of the approach that had then been adopted to deal with the highway problem, namely an increase in the size of the network. As he had in the *Tallahassee Democrat*, Buchanan explained building new roads *might* – but will probably not – work in the long run but it would "provide no relief within the immediate future" (1952b: 97). In the short run, the size of the network was given – because it takes time to build roads, because the resources that could be invested were scarce, as it was the case in 1952, or because there were places in which it was physically difficult to develop infrastructure, as in cities (97). One should thus take the supply of roads as given and find out how to allocate drivers across a network of a given size. Like Knight and Pigou before him, Buchanan treated the problem as one of misallocation of resources on a given number of roads.

However, what Buchanan emphasized was different: Congestion was not a problem of using roads of different types but using roads at different moments, being "essentially a peak-load problem" (98). Therefore, "the highway problem," added Buchanan, was "essentially one of peak load" (106). As a consequence, one could no longer conclude that infrastructures were insufficient. To the contrary, they "are more than adequate" (98) but "too large in off-peak periods" (106) and "too small in peak periods" (106). Any investments made to increase the network with the objective "to reduce congestion to acceptable proportions in peak traffic periods" would miss the point. It would not solve the problem and even be a waste of resources – "some highway resources would be wasted in off-peak periods" (106). What should rather be done was to find a way to re-allocate the demand for roads, the traffic, from peak to off-peak periods.

The number of vehicles could be rationed "directly" by "government units" – that would mean the "outright prohibition of some types of vehicles and the imposition of limitations upon other types" (98). A "more appropriate and effective means ... lies in the utilization of the rationing device of the free economy, namely price" (98). The objective – and the solution to the highway problem the USA were facing – "lie[d] in increased user charges, not to finance needed expansion, but to limit usage of the roads" (107). To him, this was obvious: "[u]nless steps of this kind are taken, congestion will continue to represent an unsolved problem" (107).

What would the price be for highway services that would "eliminate the most obvious of the congestion evils" (97) and that would allow one to "operat[e] the road and street system in a more efficient manner" (97)? Buchanan answered the question in two steps. He first warned his readers that one should not confuse prices and taxes – more precisely, "highway taxes as taxes" and "highway taxes as prices" (98). The practice consisted in viewing taxes as taxes not as prices, financing the infrastructure rather than as a means for rationing demand. As a consequence, taxes were spread across users and nonusers alike according to a benefit principle – "[t]his is the one area in which taxation on the principle of benefit received has been almost universally accepted" (98). From this perspective, beneficiaries were expected to pay a certain price or tax rate "to compensate for benefits received" (108). For instance, the driver of "a new and efficient vehicle does 'benefit' more from highways than does the motorist who drives the 'Model A'" (108). But that was not enough to have "economically 'correct' prices" (98). That was precisely the second step Buchanan made.

To do that, Buchanan emphasized that "[h]ighway services are not made available to users in discrete units" (99). Thus, "a price set too low" (99) would not reduce the demand but would generate congestion and decrease the quality of the services – "[c]ongestion prevents no motorist from traveling; it merely causes the units of highway services which he receives to be of an inferior quality" (99). Now, the problem was that "[t]he progressive deterioration in quality of highway service as congestion increases does not impinge directly on the marginal users. Rather it is primarily a 'spillover' costs represented in poorer service provided all users" (100). Thus, Buchanan had understood that congestion generates a problem of social cost – drivers impose costs on others that they should pay.[6]

---

[6] Coase (1993: 250) argued that Knight's "Fallacies in the Interpretation of Social Cost" (1924) was a major inspiration for his "The Problem of Social Cost" (1960). He even regarded his argument "as a natural extension of Knight's intuition" (1993: 250). Buchanan referred to Knight (1924) eight years before Coase's article was published and four years before Coase moved to Virginia.

In those years, none of the major contributions on the problem of social cost, on externalities and public goods, and on market failures had been published. The references in a discussion of a social cost problem remained Pigou and Knight, to whom Buchanan returned. Unsurprisingly he agreed with Knight and was against Pigou, arguing that a price should be charged on users but also insisted to take into account the spillover costs – the "correct price" for highway services correspond "to the marginal social cost incurred in providing a unit of that type of service" (100). Thus, even if "it is extremely difficult to place accurate estimates on the magnitude of these indirect costs, certain rough conclusions may be made" (100). For instance, the driver of a "Model A" should not pay a higher price because he receives higher benefits but "because he adds more to social cost" (108). Also, prices should be:

> higher on the much travelled or primary routes than on secondary roads ... greater in urban areas than in rural, and perhaps increase with population as well as traffic density ... much greater on week ends and holidays on egress routes from urban centers ... much greater during morning and evening rush hours than during midday or night hours. (100–101)

He then concluded: "[a] structure of prices incorporating the above differentials would represent a close approximation to the ideal one" (101).

The result could be achieved, Buchanan agreed, by using tolls. It would reduce congestion. However, by contrast with what Knight argued and as Frederic Benham (1934a) had noted, approaching the ideal structure of price by using tolls would probably be difficult. Buchanan explained that the system would have to be "comprehensive and highly differentiated," which would make it "completely unworkable from an administrative point of view and would be uneconomic besides" (1952b: 102). It would be more efficient to use a gasoline tax – that "serves as a rough equivalent to a mileage toll" (103) – and motor vehicle license fees – to include elements such as vehicle weight, the type of road used, and the time at which vehicle travels. Buchanan added, without giving details, that "tax financing should be considered ... to cover the total costs of construction and maintenance" (100).

Defined in this way, the price for highway services would vary from one individual to the other, which made sense for Buchanan since the benefits received by each individual were different. Another reason was that the costs each motorist generated, and that had to be covered by the price, were different. There were the costs of highway depreciation that depended on the type of vehicle used and, most importantly, the costs imposed on others. Indeed, Buchanan pointed out, using highways generated "spillover" effects. Thus, the user charge had to be set at the level of the marginal *social* cost. Users would also have to pay the "spillover" costs resulting from "[t]he progressive deterioration in quality of highway service as congestion increases" that were "represented in poorer service provided [sic] all users" (1952a: 100). Thus, for instance, "The motorist who drives a new and efficient vehicle does 'benefit' more from highways than does the motorist who drives the 'Model A'. But the latter should pay a higher price because he adds more to social cost" (108).

With this paper, Buchanan built a framework that allowed him to model the intuition he had worked on in his 1941 master essay: Users should pay. He now could add what he had learned by reading Wicksell and other economists: Users should pay a price equal to the marginal social cost in order to include the costs they impose on others. And he had no doubt that people would pay. After all, they benefit from using roads. This meant, to put it differently, that voluntary exchange theory could indeed be used to address an important empirical problem, provided that spillover effects were not forgotten and that prices were set at the level of the marginal social cost. A second point of importance in this paper is that Buchanan acknowledged the existence of a problem of social cost in the use of roads – this was, again, before Coase and was original in the early 1950s. And, at the same time, Buchanan argued that the problem could be solved quite easily – individuals do pay for the costs they impose on others. This was the first of his work on externalities and the problem of social cost.

2.4 More on Pricing, Highways, and Social Costs

2.4.1 Buchanan at RAND: Externalities and Highways

In 1954, Buchanan spent the summer in Santa Monica at the RAND Corporation. His decision to go there was largely motivated by the presence there of two of his friends – Malcolm Hoag and Roland McKean. And, logically enough, Buchanan began his stay by first reading the memos McKean had written for RAND. It was a way for Buchanan to familiarize himself with the economics of RAND. McKean was also someone with whom Buchanan could discuss issues in public finance. It was after reading these works that Buchanan wrote his first memo for RAND (M-3467). It was on July 13. Four pages about externalities and market failures.

Buchanan referred to the scarce literature on externalities that existed – including a 1954 Scitovky article. He also distinguished pecuniary effects from technological or physical external effects, as Scitocksy had done, but unlike Scitocksy he noted that only technological or physical effects would give birth to problems of social cost. The difference with Scitovsky is interest-ing – it evidences the originality of Buchanan's views, but also that it is worth noting that Buchanan emphasized the existence of a problem of social cost. And noted the failure of market mechanisms. More precisely, when projects or investments generate interdependences that "are not expressed by the market mechanism" like when external effects are technological, the market mechanism is "deficient": "We can't rely on the market to tell us that the social income has increased" (3). Indeed, the "test" that should be made to decide whether a project was socially beneficial and desirable was the "test of whether gains offset losses is no longer to be relied on" (3). Thus, "there is no assurance that compensation to losers *could* be made, even should we desire to make them" (3; emphasis on original). But, at the same time, Buchanan defended the capacity of the market system to solve this problem. Why? Because, "[t]he market ensures us that compensations could, in fact, be paid from pecuniary or market losses" (3) – the need to use "full compensation" would come back·repeatedly in Buchanan's future work.

This required that gains would compensate losses, and therefore meant that it was crucial to calculate costs and benefits "properly" (3) and compare them at a sufficiently general level. Here, Buchanan introduced another interesting idea: Projects should not be valued at their "full costs" but at the cost of their alternative use. Or, put differently, in the evaluation of public projects, "we should always consider opportunity costs" (2). Even if he did not elaborate much on that, it was there fifteen years before *Cost and Choice* (1969). This short memo written in the summer of 1954 was indeed announcing important innovations.

After having made these remarks on externalities and the problem of social cost, Buchanan decided to work again on highways, encouraged by Hoag himself who asked him to "elaborate [the] suggestion [he had made] that the general field of highway economics provides an appropriate field for the application of RAND-type research."

It is true that highways remained topical in the mid- 1950s. In May 1954, the Federal-Aid Highway Act authorized an expenditure of $175 million for interstate highways. It was "one effective forward step," Eisenhower said signing the Act, but only a step. This is also what Richard Nixon – on behalf of Eisenhower who could not attend the meeting – told the State governors gathered in Lake George, New York on July 12: The legislation signed a few months earlier was a "good start," but a more comprehensive interstate network of highways was needed. Eisenhower had a "Grand Plan," a $101 billion program to create an articulated highway system.[7] Asked to make suggestions to improve the

---

[7] Spending money was not only motivated by the need to improve the highway system. Apparently, Eisenhower also believed that a recession was threatening the US economy. Clay: "Sherman Adams called me down. This was in August 1954. We had lunch with the President, and they were concerned about the economy. We were facing a possible recession, and he wanted to have

highway network, the governors set up a Special Highway Committee.[8] Then, the president established a second Committee – an Advisory Committee in September the National Highway Program – to work out the details of how to finance the Grand Plan. Chaired by General Lucius D. Clay – chairman of the board of the Continental Can Company and a member of General Motors' board – its objective was to find "a self-liquidating method of financing that would avoid debt" (Weingroff 1996).

On August 6, Buchanan drafted a memorandum tellingly entitled "The Need for Research in Highway Economics." The memorandum was distributed on August 10, without title.[9] Among other things, Buchanan insisted on the need to take into account that highways were "a publicly produced good" that is used by automobiles, which are a "privately produced good." To put in terms Buchanan will soon use, the production and ownership of the good is centralized while its use is decentralized. This "unique" feature "creates difficult adjustment problems" between the "private productivity and social productivity of highway usage." Actually, private and social productivity differ. And this implies, Buchanan noted, that there would be "more than the socially optimum number of automobiles." Or, even if he did not use the expression then, that there was a problem of social cost. A problem that was reinforced by the spillover costs and benefits of highway usage and development, by which Buchanan meant that building and relocating new highways would in all likelihood generate costs (and possibly benefits) to property owners.

2.4.2 The Road Case Re-examined: Buchanan vs Pigou and Knight

After these weeks at RAND, Buchanan went back to Florida and started to write a book on highways, *Traffic, Tolls and Taxes: The Economics of the Nation's Highway Problem* (1955c). It would be a book for decision-makers, for "the intelligent non-economist" (1955c: pn, 1), the "large ... group of individuals who will make policy and influence decisions on highways" (pn, 1), and "not ... primarily for the professional economist" (pn, 1).[10] He had not forgotten that,

---

something on the books that would enable us to move quickly if we had to go into public works. He felt that a highway program was very important.", Smith (1990), *Lucius D. Clay: An American Life* (Holt).

[8] Headed by Governor Walter Kohler, Jr., of Wisconsin, the Committee presented its report to the President at the White House on December 3: 1954.

[9] Memorandum M-3978, August 10, 1954, to M. W. Hoag, BP, The RAND Corporation, 1953–1954, Box: 84, Folder: 2.

[10] The pages are numbered by chapter. We indicate the number of the chapter first and then the page in the chapter. "pn" means prefatory note. The second chapter – "Concrete Foundations" – in which Buchanan was supposed to discuss data and statistics about highways does not exist in the archive.

a few months earlier, he had participated in the organization of a conference with the objective to communicate with the engineers working for the highway planning agencies.[11] These men, argued Buchanan, "have come to realize the need for an understanding of the economics of the highway in the broad sense" (pn, 2).

In the course of the writing, Buchanan faced some theoretical problems that needed clarification. Thus, in November, as he was writing the chapter dealing with spillovers and externalities, Buchanan realized that he could write "an addendum"[12] or "A Digression for Economists"[13] as he entitled it. He had to develop an analysis about the problem of social cost. He thus started "a note on the old road case as spelled out by Pigou–Knight–Kahn and others."[14] The task proved to be more difficult than expected. Buchanan "hit a theoretical tanglewood,"[15] facing "one of the most complicated and slippery theoretical traps ever encountered."[16] To get out of the trap, Buchanan wrote notes which he expanded upon until they became "a full-length paper," of which he then wrote four successive versions entitled "Private Ownership and Common Usage: The Road Case Re-examined," that was eventually published in 1956.[17]

Buchanan's starting point was a practical problem: How to determine "the proper amount of the nation's economic resources which should be devoted both to the utilization and the construction of the highway system" (1)? Answering the question required taking into account "external diseconomies in the consumption or utilization of highway services" (2). And this implied that "the prices of highway services be set equal to the marginal social costs of providing such services" (1954d, 6). Or, in other words, that the price "includes the incremental costs (or reduced enjoyments) imposed upon other road users!" (6) This was the conclusion Buchanan had put forward in his 1952 article on highway services.

---

[11] In 1953, Buchanan helped organizing a conference on Highway Economics. Summarizing the objectives of the conference, he repeated that it aimed at "implementing more effective cooperation between highway agencies and universities in the economic aspects of highway development." (Buchanan, "Highway Economics Conference. Notes for Working Committee," Draft, January 14, 1954, BP.)

[12] Buchanan to Hoag, November 17, 1954, BP, Hoag, Malcolm, 1954–1968, Box: 52, Folder: 11.

[13] Buchanan to Hoag, December 12, 1954, BP, Hoag, Malcolm, 1954–1968, Box: 52, Folder: 11.

[14] Buchanan to Jenkins, November 12, 1954, BP, Jenkins, H.P.B., 1954–1955, Box: 57, Folder: 12.

[15] Buchanan to Hoag, November 17, 1954, Hoag, Malcolm, 1954–1968, Box: 52, Folder: 11.

[16] Buchanan to Jenkins, November 12, 1954, BP, Jenkins, H.P.B., 1954–1955, Box: 57, Folder: 12.

[17] The notes are undated but can reasonably be said to precede the writing of the paper. The reasoning and the argument are the same and a few similar sentences are found in the preliminary versions of the article. In the archives, there are four drafts, that go from very preliminary to very close to the final and published version. They are undated too but, in three of them, Buchanan thanked Hoag, McKean, and Collberg, which indicates that they were written after he had received their comments. We refer to them as 1954e-1, 1954e-2, 1954e-3, and 1954e-4.

The difference with his previous article – which had led him to write the addendum – was the conviction Buchanan now had that switching from public to private property would not solve the problem of social cost. In other words, Buchanan diverged from, and questioned, Knight's analysis, which had never been done before – "Professor Knight's arguments have never been seriously questioned, and indeed, I have myself implicitly accepted it in specific reference to the road example" (1954b: 1; 1954e-2). Indeed, Buchanan insisted, Knight's analysis was "perhaps misleading" (1954d: 4), "incomplete" (1954b: 8), or "not valid" (1954b: 2). Misleading or invalid, according to Buchanan, for leading his readers to think that private ownership and competition could solve the problem of social cost. Incomplete, because in his demonstration that "in a regime of private ownership prices would tend to be so adjusted as to insure the optimum allocation of economic resources, distributional effects being neglected" (1954e-4: 1), Knight had "glossed over or neglected," or "largely overlooked" "[s]everal interesting and complex points" (1954e-3: 2), which were actually "[t]he special problems created by common usage" (2). Knight indeed did "not carry through to the case of utilization or consumption interdependence" (1954b: 8).

Buchanan made his demonstration by comparing the case of roads and the allocation of labor to different types of lands, which was the example used by Knight in 1924. In his analysis, Knight had assumed that the case in which the landowner hires labor is equivalent to the case when each worker hires the land. The equivalence, Buchanan added, may hold if workers "hire the use of discrete units" of land. But it no longer holds if workers are not able to hire the use land in discrete and separable physical units, which is what happens when there exists interdependence between workers. In that case, they are only "allowed to purchase rights to contribute to and share equally in the total product" (1954e-3: 4). Then, as more rights are sold, the share each worker receives decreases. This is exactly what common usage – roads or "other commonly-used resources areas ... fishing grounds, hunting preserves, oil pools, water reserves" (21) – meant and what Knight had missed: Truck firms buy "the right to use the road along with an undetermined number of other truckers" (7). As the number of drivers increases, the space each of them is allowed to use decreases and therefore the productivity of each driver or truck decreases. But no one takes into account his impact on others or, put differently, each driver ignores that "in purchasing a share of the highway reduces the productivity of shares to all other truckers" (7).

This conclusion also meant that market pricing does not take into account external (dis)economies or spillover costs (or benefits) – "nowhere in the pricing process are the external diseconomies of usage included" (7). More precisely, when "interdependence is present these [private enjoyments] tend to be greater than social marginal enjoyments" (5). Therefore, a competitive price would not be optimal. Buchanan insisted: "When there exist external diseconomies in utilization ... competitive pricing could never take into account the spillover effects" (1954d: 3). Hence, "competitive pricing does not lead to an optimum" (3) and "[i]n the presence of either external economies or diseconomies of consumption, the competitive economy should not appear to allocate resources properly" (1954b, 2). Or, "the conclusion that the market will produce the optimum allocation is neither evident nor necessarily true except under certain explicitly defined conditions" (1954e-4: 4; 1954e-1: 3). The result was not new – "there is general agreement that the market does not produce the optimum allocation of economic resources when technological external diseconomies are present" (1954e-1: 6; e2: 8; e3: 7).

What did it mean in the case of roads? To Knight, competition meant private property, because competition takes place between potential owners. Unlike Knight, Buchanan did not believe that the solution consisted in switching from one type of property to another:

> [i]n so far as external diseconomies arise from an expansion in usage of a whole resource ... it is clear that ownership changes alone will not be sufficient. Only in those cases where the extent of the commonality of usage is limited to a relatively small proportion of the total resource supply ... can ownership rearrangements be exclusively relied upon to produce desirable results. (1954e-2: 19–20)

The institutional arrangement that would allow an optimal allocation of resources would combine a form of ownership of the resource and a type of pricing.

2.4.3 Which Institution to Implement Prices?

Here, an important difference exists between the first three drafts and the final published version of the paper. Until the last version, Buchanan compared two institutional arrangements: competitive (decentralized) ownership and operation, and centralized ownership and operation. He rejected the decentralized, competitive solution. To Buchanan, a competitive operation of roads that would lead to competitive pricing for the use of roads and competitive (decentralized) ownership – the "institutional arrangement implicit in Professor Knight's argument" (1954e-4: 16) was actually not "possible in the specific road example" (16) and would not generate an optimal allocation of resources. The social costs would not be taken into account. The solution, rather, consisted in an institutional arrangement combining centralized ownership and centralized operation.

Buchanan explained that centralized private ownership *alone* – if roads were operated privately – "would produce utilization of the resource much closer to the socially desirable one than would the treatment of the resource as a free good" (1954e-3: 15). But that would not be sufficient. It would work if the firm was sufficiently large enough to internalize the spillover costs and benefits (16). Similarly, centralized operation *alone* would work if "the commonly-used resource is priced so as to reflect the marginal 'supply' costs" (20) – by which he meant social costs. Hence, "both ownership and operation of commonly-used resources must be centralized in order for optimum resource allocation to be readily attained" (1954e-3: 20).

The problem with this conclusion was that it implied a critique of Knight, Pigou, and Kahn. And Buchanan did not like that – "I have been extremely reluctant to challenge some of the giants who have discussed the problem."[18] It meant that either he or they were right, there was no other way. On November 12, Buchanan wrote to one of his friends, Harry Jenkins, "I have about come to the 'thee and me' stage ... The further I went, the more misty and fuzzy either I or the accepted analysis became."[19] On November 17, he made the same point to Hoag: "try as I may, I cannot reconcile the accepted arguments with what appears to me to be correct."[20] Buchanan acknowledged that he might indeed be wrong – "Maybe am I off the deep end again."[21] But he might be right, in which case "the argument may be worth preparation as a separate journal article."[22] Buchanan was "pretty much confused," "so confused that I think just about everybody is crazy" and "not at all sure of anything anymore." He needed Hoag's "advice and counsel," asking him to "tell me where I am off base if I am and give me your general criticism of the manuscript." Hoag and McKean, to whom Hoag had forwarded the paper, sent back comments on December 1.

Neither Hoag nor McKean were convinced by Buchanan's analysis. Hoag did not understand how Buchanan could derive his conclusion from his

---

[18] Buchanan to Hoag, November 17, 1954, BP, Hoag, Malcolm, 1954–1968, Box: 52, Folder: 11. That's an interesting quote. Was Buchanan really reluctant to challenge all the giants? It was not uncommon for Buchanan to have doubts about what he was writing (we'll see this again in the controversy with Samuelson, to which we'll return later). He was therefore extremely cautious when unsure of his conclusions. This caution may well have led him to hesitate to criticize the giants he was talking about. It may also be that he did not want to give the impression of criticizing Knight. In any case, this reticence did not apply to all the great economists he discussed. He didn't hesitate, for example, to criticize Pigou or Keynes, but Knight was another matter. These sentences could therefore have been a form of caution.

[19] Buchanan to Jenkins, November 12, 1954, BP, Jenkins, H.P.B., 1954–1955, Box: 57, Folder: 12.

[20] Buchanan to Hoag, November 17, 1954, BP, Hoag, Malcolm, 1954–1968, Box: 52, Folder: 11.

[21] Buchanan to Jenkins, November 12, 1954, BP, Jenkins, H.P.B., 1954–1955, Box: 57, Folder: 12.

[22] Buchanan to Hoag, November 17, 1954, BP, Hoag, Malcolm, 1954–1968, Box: 52, Folder: 11.

analysis – "your argument does not establish enough of a case for saying that centralized ownership alone would not be enough."[23] This led him to doubt that Buchanan's case against Knight was "important enough or solid enough to warrant special argumentative treatment." To be clear, Hoag doubted that the point Buchanan analyzed "does not deserve the full-fledged treatment which you are proposing to give it as a separate paper." This response came from the fact that Hoag did not seem to grasp the importance of spillovers, external diseconomies as a consequence of interdependence, which he compared to "the case of a farmer coming into a market producing a product for which there is an inelastic demand, and therefore decreasing the total revenues of farmers producing that product. It is right that he should not take that interdependence into account." Buchanan's "no!" in the margin indicates his disagreement.

McKean, for his part, believed that Buchanan's paper was "very useful"[24] because it bore on a "relatively unexplored territory." But also that it

> need not, and should not be presented as quarrels with the "giants" in the profession. The important thing is not that Knight and Pigou chose an unfortunate illustration, not that Knight (like everyone else) failed to explore fully the implications of uncertainty in this connection. The important thing is, rather, that the implications of various institutional arrangements, especially in view of uncertainty and dynamic considerations, need to be traced out more fully than they have been. (emphasis in original)

Second, McKean "fe[lt] uneasy about" the conclusion. Common-pool problems were quite frequent – "common usage of atmosphere affected by the glue factory, of light-waves affected by offensive billboards, of underground drainage, of hunting and fishing areas, of a pool of trained specialists." If it were misunderstood, it could be misused and lead to more government intervention – "I should hate to contemplate governmental or monopoly ownership and operation of all these commonly-used pools." Consequently, he urged Buchanan to be cautious – "All I am suggesting is that the point be presented with extreme care, for its implications could easily be overextended." Buchanan partially, even if cautiously, incorporated Hoag's and McKean's comments on "The Road Case." He did not abandon the criticisms against the "giants" that had troubled him.[25] But, between him and them, he had chosen. In the published version of the paper, Buchanan repeated that Knight had

---

[23] Hoag to Buchanan, December 1, 1954, BP, Hoag, Malcolm, 1954–1968, Box: 52, Folder: 11.

[24] McKean to Buchanan, December 1, 1954, BP, "Unofficial Academic Letters", 1957–1970, Box: 102, Folder: 6.

[25] On February 15, Buchanan sent Hoag another version, noting "I am not sure of anything on this subject any more." Buchanan to Hoag, February 15, 1955, BP, Hoag, Malcolm, 1954–1968, Box: 52, Folder: 11.

misunderstood the main characteristics of roads and that his argument about the possibility to allocate resources efficiently in the presence of externalities or spillovers by changing the ownership of the resource did not hold. But Buchanan nonetheless followed McKean's advice when he changed his conclusions about the importance of public ownership to solve the problem of social cost characterizing roads. He introduced a third institutional arrangement comparing single (or centralized) ownership and monopoly pricing of the resource services, with competitive (decentralized) ownership and competitive pricing of road services, as well as competitive ownership and monopoly pricing.

Buchanan explained that centralized ownership and monopoly pricing were as problematic as competitive pricing and operation, both leading to an inefficient use of roads. It was actually the third institutional arrangement that should be chosen – "Only in the intermediate pattern in which competitive ownership prevails but monopoly pricing principles are followed are the results consistent with efficiency criteria when interdependence among user decisions is present" (1956a: 315). However Buchanan stuck to his claim about marginal cost pricing, noting that this could be realized when "the government . . . owns the roads and price the road services at the level of marginal social cost" (315). The paper was ready and submitted by mid-March 1955[26] and published in 1956.

3 Buchanan's Beliefs about Individualized Prices Put to the Test

3.1 Samuelson's Condition

Buchanan was writing on market failures, on the problem of social cost, and on institutional solutions for implementing competitive pricing of road services when "The Pure Theory of Public Expenditure" (1954) was published. This is not only one of Samuelson's most important articles, it was also a major challenge to Buchanan. Samuelson's views were close and opposed to those of Buchanan.

On a general level, Samuelson's objective was identical to Buchanan's. He wanted to build a pure theory of government finance, and Buchanan had also contemplated developing one himself – one remembers the title of Buchanan's 1949 article: "The Pure Theory of Government Finance: A Suggested Approach" (1949a). That said, Samuelson was moving in a totally different direction than the one chosen by Buchanan. The latter claimed that public

---

[26] On March 15, Buchanan sent the paper to the *Quarterly Journal of Economics*. On June 1, Edward Chamberlain informed him that the paper was not accepted. Then, Buchanan submitted it to the *American Economic Review*, and after it had been rejected again, to the *Southern Economic Journal* where he was finally accepted, "with enthusiasm" (Schwenning to Buchanan, August 22, 1955, BP, "Private Ownership and Common Usage: The Road Case Reexamined" drafts and correspondence, 1954–1956, Box: 190, Folders: 14 and 15).

expenditure and taxation should be treated together. For his part, Samuelson insisted that they could be decoupled and claimed that a theory of government should be based on an analysis of public expenditure rather than on taxation – which was what most economists have studied: "Except for Sax, Wicksell, Lindahl, Musgrave, and Bowen, economists have rather neglected the theory of optimal public expenditure, spending most of their energy on the theory of taxation" (Samuelson 1954: 387; see also 1958: 332).

A second more specific element also attracted Buchanan's attention, the nature of goods that Samuelson analyzed in his model. Samuelson's (1954) article is about public or collective consumption goods and their impact on the allocation of resources. These goods are, to Samuelson, such that all individuals "enjoy in common in the sense that each individual's consumption of such good leads to no subtraction from any other individual's consumption of that good" (1954: 387). Samuelson explained that this assumption allowed one to introduce in the public finance theory a "vital" (1955: 350) element, namely "external economies" or "external interdependencies that no theory of government can do without" (350). Samuelson, thus, did not distinguish public goods from goods that produce externalities as Buchanan had done. Buchanan treated roads as public goods with spillover effects.

Samuelson had the same objective as Buchanan and was also dealing with the same issues. But Samuelson did not reach the same conclusions as Buchanan *at all*. These conclusions were encapsulated in the three conditions Samuelson famously established to be satisfied to reach a Pareto-optimal allocation of resources in an economy with private and pure public goods. There was, first, the standard optimality condition for private goods. Second, Samuelson added a specific condition for public goods, "which constitutes a pure theory of government expenditure on collective consumption goods" (1954: 388), which was at the same time sufficient and necessary: The sum of the individual marginal rates of substitution between a public good and any private good should be equal to a unique marginal rate of transformation between those two goods. Then, he also included a third condition, based on a social welfare function (SWF) to determine how much each individual would pay, a condition that summarized the "normative judgments concerning the relative ethical desirability of different configurations involving some individuals being on a higher level of indifference and some on a lower" (387).

Samuelson's third conclusion is important because of the point on normative judgments in economics. Resorting to a SWF also came from the impossibility to use individualized prices, or taxes, for public goods – at least not according to individual benefits:

taxing according to a benefit theory of taxation can not at all solve the computational problem in the decentralized manner possible for the first category of "private" goods to which the ordinary market pricing applies and which do not have the "external effects" basic to the very notion of collective consumption goods. (389)

By extension, marginal social cost pricing could not be used for pure public goods. The difference with Buchanan could hardly be greater.

The impossibility to use individualized prices went hand in hand with the impossibility to use markets or a market mechanism to reach an optimal allocation of resources in the presence of public goods. Indeed, Samuelson claimed that one could not use decentralized mechanisms to lead individuals to pay a price corresponding to his marginal rate of substitution between a private and a public good. He insisted: "*No* decentralized pricing system can serve to determine optimally these levels of collective consumption" (388; emphasis in original). In fact, no decentralized mechanism would work. The "'Scandinavian consensus,' Kant's 'categorical imperative,' other devices meaningful only under conditions of 'symmetry'" were in his view "utopian" (389).

Samuelson gave two reasons to explain what he called the "failure of market catallactics" (389). First, marginal cost pricing could not be used for public goods or in the case of decreasing costs because it would lead to prices equal to zero (Desmarais-Tremblay 2016: 133). That technical condition was certainly less important than the behavioral one he introduced in his analysis, namely that marginal (social) cost pricing worked only if individuals revealed their true preferences about the quantity of collective goods they want to consume or, as Samuelson put, were "indoctrinated to behave like a 'parametric decentralized bureaucrat' reveals his preferences by signaling in response to price parameters or Lagrangean multiplies to questionnaires, or to other devices" (1954: 389). But, to Samuelson, even such an indoctrination could not resist that "hope to snatch some selfish benefits" (389). Samuelson shared Musgrave's pessimistic views on human nature. He was convinced that individuals would not reveal their preferences. He thus wrote: "It is in the selfish interest of each person to give *false* signals, to pretend to have less interest in a given collective consumption activity than he really has" (388–389).

3.2 Buchanan's Condition: A Defense of Individualized Prices

In December 1954, Buchanan attended the *American Economic Association* (AEA) conference in Detroit, where he met Musgrave and Julius Margolis who was putting together ideas to write critical comments on Samuelson (Margolis 1955). They discussed Samuelson's paper. Either Buchanan had started reading the article before meeting Margolis and Musgrave or they incited him to do so but, in any case, Buchanan finished reading Samuelson's paper by the end of January on the 25th. Buchanan wrote Margolis: "I have finally gotten around to reading Samuelson's note which we discussed with Musgrave in Detroit."[27] And had found that Samuelson had made a "fundamental mistake." Buchanan decided to postpone revising "The Road Case," to "hurriedly" write a comment, a "little note which . . . develops [his] initial reaction to the Samuelson note."[28] Cautious, Buchanan first sent his essay to Margolis. He wanted to know if his claim was "substantially correct, and if it is a completely separate point from those that you develop."[29] He was, did he add, "not sure at all that it is right."[30] Margolis's reply confirmed that Buchanan's doubts were well founded. Although he found that Buchanan's "note certainly expands on Samuelson and illuminates his article,"[31] Margolis nonetheless did not believe that Buchanan included anything new to solve the problem Samuelson was trying to solve. In particular, there was nothing original when compared to Samuelson:

> your condition 2a is not a condition of optimality but is instead a condition necessary to achieve the optimum if we were to rely on a decentralized 'pricing' system. Though Samuelson does not specify 2a in a literary fashion he states the equivalent and he further claims that the absence of this condition is what makes the voluntary exchange theory incorrect.[32]

Yet this initial reaction did not discourage Buchanan from moving forward. In early February, he sent Samuelson almost exactly – the differences are minor – the "Note on a Pure Theory of Public Expenditure" that he sent to Margolis to check if his claims were not "off base somewhere."[33] And the core of his note was this "condition 2a" Margolis referred to in his letter. This was precisely the condition Buchanan had added to complement Samuelson's analysis and upon which rested all their disagreement.

According to Buchanan, Samuelson was wrong because he reasoned in aggregate terms to determine a Pareto optimal allocation of resources. The use of a "unique marginal rate of substitution in production" and therefore the abandonment of individualized prices for the public was problematic. This meant that he had abandoned price discrimination – "the relative 'prices' of collective and private goods are made uniform for all individuals." Removing price discrimination for private goods was "a step toward Pareto optimality" (3), as consumers can adjust their consumption to equalize their marginal rate of

---

[27] Buchanan to Margolis, January 25, 1955. [28] Buchanan to Margolis, January 25, 1955.
[29] Buchanan to Margolis, January 25, 1955. [30] Buchanan to Margolis, January 25, 1955.
[31] Margolis to Buchanan, February 2, 1955. [32] Margolis to Buchanan, February 2, 1955.
[33] Buchanan to Samuelson, February 9, 1955, BP, Series 3: Writings, Box: 196, Folder: 2.

substitution between two private goods to the relative price of these goods. But it was a step *away* from Pareto optimality when there are public goods because individuals cannot adjust their consumption of public goods. A unique marginal rate of substitution meant that all individuals would pay the same price for the public good, independently from their preference for the good. Those who make little or no use of the public good are paid the same as those who extensively consume it. One could even envisage that one individual or a few to bear the entire cost of provision of the public good.[34] Indeed: "It is true the summation of individual exchange ratios must be equal to the 'social' exchange ratio. But this does not allow the individual differences to be neglected, since there are many possible ways of adding up" (5). Therefore, an allocation of resources reached under Samuelson conditions – based on this unique exchange ratio – could hardly be optimal.

Thus, the prices for public goods should be individualized to allow an adjustment impossible to achieve through quantities. This was why Buchanan added an *individual* condition – the so-called condition 2a – to guarantee an optimal provision of public goods. Buchanan's individual condition was the usual optimality condition for private goods extended to public goods. This condition stated that the cost of acquiring collective goods differs from one individual to the other and should correspond to the amount each individual is willing to pay for the good to guarantee a Pareto allocation of resources. Put differently, for each individual the relative of price of a public good in terms of a private good should equal the marginal rate of substitution between these two goods. To guarantee an optimal allocation of resources with private and public goods, Buchanan wrote, "each individual must equate the marginal rate of substitution in consumption between any collective good and one private good with the marginal rate of substitution between these two goods in produc-tion *to him*" (4; emphasis in original). Then, each individual would be certain to be on "his own utility frontier."[35]

Buchanan admitted that his condition was not necessary in two situations. First, if "the cost of acquiring collective goods is the same for each individual" (1955c: 6). This means that the differences between individuals are neglected, and the marginal rates of substitutions can be assumed to be identical for each individual and the same "prices" can be charged to each individual. Then, Samuelson's condition was necessary and sufficient. Otherwise, the individual-ist condition must be added to the Samuelson condition. But Buchanan believed that there was no situation in which all the individuals could be charged an

---

[34] Buchanan to Samuelson, March 4, 1955, BP, Series 3: Writings, Box: 196, Folder: 2.
[35] Buchanan to Samuelson, March 4, 1955, BP, Series 3: Writings, Box: 196, Folder: 2.

identical price. His condition was necessary. Second, Buchanan's individual condition was "not needed in the Samuelson formulation" (1955a: 7), in a frame in which exists a SWF. Given such a function, no additional individual condition was needed to say how the costs of the provision of the public good should be distributed among individuals. Individual shares were given by, and incorporated in, the SWF. However, the Buchanan condition had added became necessary for those who were "not willing move beyond the 'narrow' or Paretian version of modern welfare economics" (1). Consequently, Buchanan's condition was necessary for anyone trying to develop an "alternative" to Samuelson's welfare economics, as Buchanan did. It was *the* condition for an alternative welfare economics in which there was *no* SWF.

Buchanan's note triggered a correspondence that lasted over a year, and in which Buchanan appeared eager to reconcile their views to "advance ... an interpretation ... that serves to explain both your article and your letter as well as my note, at least to my present satisfaction."[36] Buchanan was genuinely trying to understand Samuelson, who was not to be convinced. But Buchanan kept on trying. Even when he wrote Jenkins, in May 1955, that it was over – "The little debate I started with Samuelson faded away after a few interesting exchanges. I suppose he came to the conclusion that I could not speak his language and he never seemed to understand mine"[37] – it was not. Buchanan tried again after the publication of Samuelson's "Diagrammatic Exposition of a Theory of Public Expenditure" (1955). He had finally found an answer: Samuelson's *new* argumentation could *now* be interpreted in Buchanan's way. What Samuelson now wrote meant that "not only must the Paretian frontier be attained, but also that it must be attained in a Paretian way that is, in such a way that no one is made worse off the process of reaching it" (Buchanan 1956b: 13).

Thus, Buchanan interpreted Samuelson's "Diagrammatic Exposition" as implying that a Pareto allocation could be reached if the individualist condition that he had pleaded for in his comments was satisfied: "The characteristics of the Samuelson optimal position must be emphasized. For each individual the 'marginal price' of government is equal to his marginal rate of substitution between public goods and private goods" (3). Thus, one realizes that Buchanan understood that Samuelson had eventually included Buchanan's condition in his analysis.[38] Or, put differently, Buchanan interpreted Samuelson as new

---

[36] Buchanan to Samuelson, February 25, 1955, BP, Series 3: Writings, Box: 196, Folder: 2.
[37] Buchanan to Jenkins, May 5, 1955, BP, Jenkins, H.P.B., 1954–1955, Box: 57, Folder: 12.
[38] For a detailed analysis of this debate, see Marciano 2013.

defending individualized prices. But Samuelson disagreed. He wrote Buchanan to tell him that their views differed.[39] It was a no to individualized prices.

3.3 Reaffirming the Importance of Pricing

Buchanan did not doubt that he was right to defend the pricing of public goods, despite Samuelson. Further evidence is given by what he wrote in 1955 on highways.

To start with, there was "Painless Pavements: Highways by High Finance" (1955a), "a little quib"[40] about the report the Clay Committee had presented to Eisenhower on January 11, 1955, Buchanan wrote exactly when he was writing his comment on Samuelson. The Clay Committee report claimed that the modernization and extension of the US highway system could be financed only by increasing public expenditures. To do that, it was proposed to use bonds that would be issued by the federal government but managed by a Federal Highway Corporation and not directly by the state – there was a constitutional limit on the amount of the public debt, and using a federal agency would allow bypassing the limit. In other words, the Clay Committee proposed that the investments that were supposedly needed should be financed by increasing the debt. Nothing was said about the expenditures or whether they should be controlled or limited. Nothing was said about the origins of the funds. Focusing on expenditures, and ignoring taxation, they were in line with Samuelson.

Then, on January 12, Buchanan was in Washington for a conference on highways that was organized by the Committee for Economic Development.[41] The discussion was, to Buchanan, "fine" but left him "more than ever convinced of the need for some economic analysis." Indeed, no one seemed to understand what the Clay Committee proposals, which Buchanan judged "literally fantastic," meant from an economic perspective. He felt being one of the rare who did – "I found myself in the corner alone with the representative of the American Association of Railroads on almost every issue." This was why he wrote "Painless Pavements" as he did, "in a popular vein"[42] aimed at decision-makers and not academics, with the hope that it might "exert some influence here in the

---

[39] Samuelson wrote Buchanan: "Alas, I have been so busy that I have simply not been able to find the time to give this [Buchanan's note] the attention it assuredly deserves. I did give the manuscript a quick reading the day it arrived, and it gave me the impression that your interpretation of my writings differs considerably from my own," Samuelson to Buchanan, 1956.

[40] Buchanan to Jenkins, February 11, 1955, BP, Jenkins, H.P.B., 1954–1955, Box: 57, Folder: 12.

[41] It was Hoag who helped Buchanan to be invited to the conference and to work for the Committee for Economic Development (Buchanan to Hoag, January 25, 1955, BP), on which he sat for the first semester of 1955, "selling [his] soul for $50 a day" (Buchanan to Hoag, May 23, 1955, BP, Hoag, Malcolm, 1954–1968, Box: 52, Folder: 11).

[42] Buchanan to Jenkins, February 11, 1955, BP, Jenkins, H.P.B., 1954–1955, Box: 57, Folder: 12.

right direction." The goal was also to alert the public to these issues and the fallacies the proposals conveyed.

"Painless Pavements" is as much a direct comment on the Clay Committee report as an indirect reaction to Samuelson's article. Significantly, Buchanan ignored the violation of the constitutional rules that the Clay Committee proposal implied. He only targeted the objective, to issue debt to finance the increase in public spending without envisaging taxing users or pricing highway services, and the separation between expenditures and revenues it implied. Buchanan thus noted how "extraordinary" (1955a: 2) was the proposal made by the committee, that would:

> more than double the annual rate of highway expenditure without an increase in the gasoline tax or in motor vehicle license fees, and the committee proudly points out that the desired objective may be attained without increasing the national debt (1–2).

The proposal was, in fact, not surprising. Buchanan noted that "these post-Keynesian years when federal spending apparently lost whatever connection it once might have had with federal revenues" (2), and Samuelson was just another example of this doctrine. Logically, both missed that it implied a magical trick – Buchanan wrote, "the Clay committee has at last discovered the fiscal version of Aladdin's wonderful lamp" (2). Issuing bonds gave the impression that financing highways was costless, that "all governmental 'good things' such as super-super highways may come to us without our having to bear either the burden of taxation or the sufferings of conscience over increasing national debt" (2). That was wrong – "good things come at a cost," Buchanan wrote, "whether they be provided by the government or the grocery store" (2).[43] In the case of public spending, issuing debt would give birth to inflation. Thus, the increase in the size of the highway network and its modernization would be paid for by inflation. And inflation was a form of taxation, "the most inequitable form ... which has ever been devised" (15). The Clay Committee ignored or forgot this side of the problem.

Then, after the criticisms, Buchanan envisaged solutions. As in his 1952 article on highway services, he insisted again that increasing the size of the

---

[43] In an unpublished paper, "The Politics of Economic Policy" (1953; see Marciano, 2021), Buchanan said that equating public and private spending was a "myth." It was now as if he was not really sure anymore. And he had not been in Italy yet, where he would discover David Ricardo's work on the equivalence between private and public debt, the works of some Italian Public Finance theorists, such as Antonio de Viti de Marco and Bevenuto Grizzioti. He had then no idea that he would write a book on public debt, *Public Principles of Public Debt. A Defense and Restatement*, in which he would make the same claim: "The analogy between public debt and private debt is fundamentally correct" (1958e: 56).

network would be useless if congestion had not been dealt with by reducing traffic first. Demand had to be rationed, which could be done by using prices (i.e., taxes) – "The answer to the whole highway problem lies in 'pricing' the highway correctly. The existence of congestion on our streets and highways is solely due to the fact that we do not charge high enough 'prices' for their use." (14) Pricing that Samuelson rejected in the case of public goods. Buchanan thus re-affirmed his main view, even if it opposed to Samuelson's. He was surprised that prices were used for all kinds of goods but for roads – "This is one of the main functions of price in our free enterprise economy ... [p]rice relieves potential congestion around our meat counters, our motels, and our models. Why do we shun its usage in the case of highway services?" (15) In addition, pricing highway services would also increase government revenues. Prices performed two functions: They would "cut the Gordian knot of congestion and would provide more than adequate revenues to finance [the] expansion" (16) of the highway system.

That was also one of the points Buchanan made in *Traffic, Tolls and Taxes* (1955c). Buchanan came back to the book after having completed "The Road Case Re-examined." Most of what Buchanan then wrote was not new. He reasserted and further developed the ideas on externalities and highways which he already stated. He repeated that increasing the size of the network would not reduce but rather reinforce congestion. Building more roads would create a vicious circle – an "expenditure race between highway spending government units and the automobile companies" (3: 21) similar to "the armaments race between the United States and Russia" (3: 1). He repeated that pricing highway services was the solution and insisted on the need to take spillover costs into account and to set the price for highway services at the level of what Buchanan called "the marginal resources cost." (5, 10; emphasis in original). The interesting point is that Buchanan wrote all of this during the controversy with Samuelson. He did not seem to doubt that, in the end, it was his view that would prevail. Or, at least, that it was his ideas that should be conveyed to the decision-makers.

As in the 1952 article, Buchanan also defended user taxes. Prices should be indirect and be raised as taxes on vehicles and fuel[44] as it was done in the USA. Thus, with his analysis, Buchanan had "provide[d] a rationalization, of sorts, for the practices actually employed by states and governmental units." (6: 5) And,

---

[44] Highways are bought in discrete units. Individuals could not pay the price for each unit of the road they use. Furthermore, users could not be charged once and for all, by paying an entrance fee, for instance. A fixed "season ticket" – as with clubs – was not suitable here. Individual contributions should relate to the use of roads. And tolls were too costly to manage. Thus, the best solution was to use "indirect" prices (3: 7).

to him, "these user taxes do represent a structure of charge which do not diverge too significantly in form from an acceptable structure once it is recognized that any sort of ideal structure is impossible" (4: 16). Although not designed for such a purpose, taxes could be viewed as serving a "pricing" function (4: 15). Such taxes serve to ration individual demand for roads and also generate the revenues required to finance the building of highways – user taxes "are designed to serve a pricing as well as a financing function" (4: 15). They solve the problem the Clay Committee, and the various US governments, had tried to solve. Or, more precisely, the current way of charging user taxes in the USA solved that problem. There was no need to resort to public debt. With his book, Buchanan was clearly planning to make a point against the Clay Committee report.

Continuing in the vein of his previous publications, Buchanan reiterated the existence of the problem of social cost, of "a genuine difference between private and social cost" (3: 12). Indeed, individuals base their decisions on the private costs and benefits of using roads or highways and ignore how "the presence of the[ir] vehicle" affects others and "increase[s] . . . [t]heir cost of movement" (3: 12). Which raises the question of the implementation of these prices. Buchanan's answer echoed arguments from "The Road Case": "the market fails to work" (5: 6); monopolies are not better, and, in addition, the highway system could be "classified as a public utility" (4: 7) since they "yield benefits to the social group as a whole" (6: 7). State intervention was therefore necessary and legitimate.

3.4 More Doubts about Individualized Prices

When Buchanan sat on the Committee for Economic Development he tried in vain to convince the other members that the pricing of highway services was a topic to which some attention should be paid. He did not manage to get the solution mentioned in the "policy statement" issued by the Committee at the end of its work – "any attempt on my part to sell them (not the staff but the committee) on the idea of rationing or limiting highway usage by price (taxes) was knocked out. It continues to be amazing how fixed the old ideas are."[45] Many were those who doubted that public goods could be priced as if they were private goods and that social cost problems could be addressed by decentralized mechanisms.

Oscar Brownlee and Walter Heller, for instance, agreed that "highway services should be priced in much the same manner as other services would be priced in a competitive market" (1956: 237). They even cited Buchanan and his 1952 article. But they also immediately noted the practical difficulty of

---

[45] Buchanan to Hoag, August 12, 1955, BP, Hoag, Malcolm, 1954–1968, Box: 52, Folder: 11.

collecting information about how motorists use highways. Therefore, to them, "deciding precisely what prices should be charged for each of the various kinds of services would prove to be a difficult [problem] to solve" (237). Brownlee made this point again in 1959 when he presented a paper at the conference on "Public Finances: Needs, Sources, and Utilization" that Buchanan co-organized (see 4.2 below). In "User Prices vs. Taxes" (1961: 421), Brownlee "favored the use of price as a means of rationing" and added that "the fact that a service has external economies associated with its consumption does not imply that it should not be priced" (425). But he cautioned that it should be done "when there is a reasonable possibility" (421) and concluded "[t]he allocation of public services by means of their pricing has limited applicability" (432).

In a 1957 article, Margolis had similar conclusions. He studied the case of an irrigation project, noting a decision about building a dam and distributing water had two dimensions. First, one had to determine the optimal size of the dam and the network. He demonstrated why "the value of the marginal product of water is equal to the marginal cost of providing the water" (1957: 451). Second, one had to price the use of the system. Among the different mechanisms that could be used, Margolis concluded that "[a] two-part, or a discriminatory, pricing system, or a combination of both, is necessary to allocate water efficiently" (462). Indeed, "it achieves the optimal output, since the price of the marginal unit purchased by each consumer equals its marginal cost" (452). He thus agreed with Buchanan. In addition, he added, this method "permit[s] projects to be financially independent and thereby autonomous" (462). He nonetheless concluded, as Brownlee, Heller, and Samuelson had, "that efficient pricing practices are unlikely" (462).

One exception was Jack Wiseman, who suggested a solution that anticipated Buchanan's theory of clubs.[46] In an article published in 1957, "The Theory of Public Utility Price-An Empty Box," Wiseman wrote that "no general pricing rule or rules can be held unambiguously to bring about an 'optimum' use of resources by public utilities, even in theory" (1957: 56). But he nonetheless argued that, despite "analytical shortcomings ... the multi-part tariff rule, both in its simple form and as modified by a 'club' principle" could work (57). "Modified" meant that the "members" (64) of the club would pay a "fixed charge," a "part of the common cost" instead of "a price per unit equal to marginal cost" (64). The club existed and the good or service provided "if the

---

[46] Sandler and Tschirhart (1980: 1482) mention Wiseman as one of "the first researchers to focus on a cost-sharing rationale for clubs in which cost per user fell over some range of membership size." They note that he "was critical of the club principle in public utility pricing" (1504), but not that Wiseman nonetheless thought that "the 'club' principle can be justified in individual cases" (1957: 73). And do not suggest a possible link with Buchanan, as we shall see below.

sum of the amounts offered would be great enough to cover the total outlays required" (64). Here, one would note, Samuelson's aggregate condition and a specific form of Buchanan's condition that looked like Wicksell's proposal – a fixed charge plus a price equal to the marginal cost – were satisfied. As in what Buchanan had written to Samuelson, there was no SWF and the amount to pay was not imposed on the individuals.

Wiseman had thus made an important step, paving the way for voluntary collective and private institutional arrangements that individuals could devise to deal with the economic problems that they could not solve privately. Indeed, the solutions to economic problems were institutional. And clubs seemed to be that institution. Wiseman qualified his purpose. Clubs could not be said to really involve voluntarism: Individuals' "agreement [is] 'voluntary' ... in the special sense that a malefactor voluntarily goes away to prison after a judge has sentenced him; he chooses the best alternative still available" (66). Only one type of clubs was acceptable in terms of voluntarism, "the *direct production club* ... created and administered by the consumers themselves." (66; emphasis in original). In that case, all "potential consumers" gather and "arrange both the amount of the good each individual shall consume and the amount that he shall pay for it" (64). They chose to act collectively and privately to finance a public good. But such type of clubs "seem[ed] unlikely to be of widespread importance" (67). Clubs were only a marginal solution to the pricing of public goods and services.

The problem thus remained entire. Even those who were more sympathetic to the use of decentralized mechanisms and of prices for public goods and services also reached a negative conclusion about the practical impossibility to use individualized prices for public goods or externalities. Which mechanism could be used? Was the intervention of the government inevitable? Or could another mode of organization of collective action not be envisaged, which would not involve government intervention, and which would be based on individuals' willingness to pay? What form would or could it take?

Answering required a theory of collective action which, at the time in the mid-to-late 1950s, Buchanan had not yet developed. Actually, collective action, rules, and institutions were not really a topic in economics. Not even for Buchanan. Rules had played such a minor role in his earlier work that it would have been surprising to see him suddenly focus on collective action. A methodological change was necessary. It was the step Buchanan took before embarking on the construction of a theory of collective action. His encounter with Rutledge Vining was crucial in this respect.

4 Virginia Political Economy, Collective Action, and Public Finance

4.1 Rules, Collective Action, and Political Economy

In his 1954 article, Samuelson not only criticized what Buchanan believed in and made a point with which Buchanan disagreed. He also indicated what had to be done to understand how to implement his condition. To "explore further the problem raised by public expenditure," he concluded, "would take us into the mathematical domain of 'sociology' or 'welfare politics', which Arrow, Duncan Black, and others have just begun to investigate" (1954: 389). And if the requirement applied to Samuelson's condition, it also applied to Buchanan's condition. But Samuelson added that the answers would not be given by political economists. Political economy was one sector in economics dealing with issues as complex as those discussed in his article, which required an approach that would transcend the boundaries of the "subsector" in economics. It is unclear if Samuelson intended to make the move, or if he suggested that economists should move in this direction. Buchanan, for his part, adopted this direction in 1957 when he created, with Nutter and Vining, the *Thomas Jefferson Center*. And even when he began to modify his research program in a way that allowed him to make room for Samuelson's suggestion.

Linking the creation of the Thomas Jefferson Center to this (unsettled) discussion between Buchanan and Samuelson may seem exaggerated. Other factors played a role too. After all, Buchanan mentioned the "minor irritations in the social fabric" that allowed the "institutions to be modified out of all recognition" (1958c: 6). One might speculate as to what these "minor irritations" were and why Buchanan seemed to minimize their importance. One might assume that he was referring to the political context in Virginia, the massive resistance against desegregation (see, e.g., McLean 2017). Buchanan did not ignore the situation (see Fleury and Marciano 2018a, 2018b). But how much it influenced the decision to create a research center remains a matter of speculation. One can hardly understand the desire to build a school of economics at the University of Virginia (UVA) without taking into account "Buchanan's scholarly program as well" (Fleury and Marciano 2018b: 1515). This is what we stress here, Buchanan's academic objectives. Among which, one finds the dissatisfaction with the kind of economics Samuelson (and others) were proposing.[47]

---

[47] For a more complete history of the creation of the Thomas Jefferson Center, with a focus on the Chicagoan roots of the project (see Medema 2009; Levy and Peart 2020; Boettke and Kroencke 2020; Boettke and Marciano 2015; Fleury and Marciano 2018a).

Buchanan, Nutter, and Vining disagreed with the economists' growing obsession with technique and the "[g]reat emphasis" economists placed "upon the mastery of technical tools" (1956–1&2: 1). It was not a question of banning the use of formal tools per se. What was problematic was when mathematical reasoning replaced economic reasoning, when normative propositions were derived from mathematical analyses despite, and even against, what an economic analysis suggested. That was the case of Kenneth Boulding and Donald Patinkin, about whom Buchanan wrote explicitly in a paper drafted between September and November 1956, for the annual conference of the Southern Economic Association and published later (1958a). And, clearly, also of Samuelson, already one of the most eminent, if not *the* eminent mathematical economists.

By contrast, Buchanan and Nutter who were convinced Knightians, had in mind to follow Knight's path.[48] They were not the only ones. At UVA Buchanan and Nutter made the acquaintance of an economist who shared their views: Vining.[49] A few months before Buchanan arrived at UVA, Vining's *Economics in the United States of America. A Review and Interpretation of Research* (1956) was published. Commissioned by UNESCO, the project involved the "charting of research activity in the social sciences throughout the world." Vining's "report" was written "to give a bird's-eye view of … recent trends in economic … research in the United States of America." Vining wrote a critical statement of what economists were doing, of their tendency to focus on means-ends problems, problems that consist in selecting the "'optimum' alternative" (16) to reach a predetermined, non-debatable, objectively quantifiable, and measurable end. This implied that, first, economists tend to focus almost exclusively on the concept of optimum or efficiency. Second, as a corollary, they were "undertak[ing] a task resembling that of the mathematical statistician for whom the concept of efficiency or optimum is fundamental" (36). A third point led them to "present [their] theor[ies] as a technical device for objectively evaluating the efficiency of an economic system" (36), and, the fourth point aimed at being used "to instruct the management upon whether or not a particular system of rules constitutes an optimum or efficient quality control system" (36). Economics was increasingly viewed as a technique aimed at telling decision-makers which rules were the most efficient to reach a well-defined end. This was, in particular, the case of welfare economists such

---

[48] "We have, I think, the makings of what could be a rather interesting little group in Buchanan, Vining, and myself – all solid Chicago products who did our lessons in Knight well," is what Nutter wrote Coase to convince him to join them at UVA in a letter he sent him on December 4, 1956. Quoted by David Levy and Sandra Peart, 2020, 18–19.

[49] On the role Vining played see Levy and Peart (2020).

as Tjalling Koopmans and Tibor Scitovsky, which Vining more precisely targeted in his book.

To Vining, this perspective was erroneous. Means-ends problems were the problems studied in engineering, natural sciences, mathematics, operations research, and so on. They should not be studied by economists. These were simply not "social problem[s]" (9). No discussion, disagreement, or conflict could exist about the ends or about the means since these variables were quantified and defined in objective terms. The social problems political economists had to deal with were those involving social conflict. Indeed, the individuals who live in a society have different goals and objectives that they try to reconcile in order to act jointly and become a society. This was done by defining "a system of rules . . . a system of legislative constraints upon individual action" (17). And choosing a system of rules was a "joint process." The constraints were chosen and "imposed by the individuals acting jointly" (34). More precisely, since these choices were actually made by the legislators "who act on behalf of the members of a society" (15), political economists had to "to assist the legislature in arriving at these judgments" (40) regarding different systems of rules. Which was, insisted Vining, exactly the perspective classical political economists such as Smith, Hume, and Ricardo had, "our conception of political economy is . . . strictly classical" (14).

The proximity of Vining's theses with Buchanan's own work was striking. Buchanan had stressed the importance of having, and studying, the rules of the game in his dissertation, but had not really pushed that aspect further since 1948. And did not deepen the connection with classical political economy. Now that Samuelson had suggested that the solution to the pricing of public goods was partly institutional, and Vining also suggested the need to adopt an institutional approach, it seemed that the time had come to develop this perspective.[50]

4.2 Public Finance and Collective Action

At the end of 1956 or in the first months of 1957, Buchanan knew that finding a way to implement his condition to guarantee an optimal allocation of resources in the presence of public goods without resorting to government intervention meant focusing on collective action. He also knew this objective was consistent with reorienting economics towards political economy, such as

---

[50] It is therefore not a surprise if they spent hours discussing Vining's essay (Levy and Peart 2020, 7). Buchanan acknowledged the importance of Vining, who "initiat[ed] what was to become a centrally important component of Virginia Political Economy, the stress on rules as contrasted with the then universal stress on policy alternatives within rules. Vining repeatedly emphasized that relevant political choices are . . . are among alternative set of rules, arrangements, or constraints" (2007: 96).

Vining had defined it in his 1956 report. Since Buchanan was and had always been a public finance theorist, he applied this new perspective to public finance theory that he began to envisage differently than before. Precisely in a way that would allow him "to explore further the problem raised by public expenditure" and, at the same time, develop a theory of collective action.

To make that step, Buchanan took advantage of an opportunity offered to him by George Stigler during the fall of 1956. Stigler proposed to Buchanan "to get up [a committee] for the National Bureau looking toward a conference in public finance"[51] and Buchanan accepted. He chaired the organizing committee, on which Roland McKean, Charles Lindblom, and Richard Musgrave served too. The conference took place in March 1959 at UVA, and the papers were gathered in a volume entitled *Public Finances: Needs, Sources, and Utilization* (1961b).

The topic of the conference was *Collective Resource Use in the United States*, which differs from the title of the book published later. Another difference with the book, in which no structure is apparent, is that each day of the conference had a specific purpose. On the first day, there were scheduled papers on the study of "Public Financial Needs: Which Government and How Much?" These papers were devoted to fiscal federalism (Musgrave and Tiebout), public finance in a multilevel structure (Lazlo Ecker-Racz), and metropolitan area finance (Margolis). The plan for the second day was to have "Decision Making in Taxation and Expenditure" (Lindblom), "Planning Defense Expenditure" (Alain Enthoven), "User Prices vs. Taxes" (Brownlee), and "Cost-Benefit Analysis" (Otto Eckstein). These papers were gathered under the theme "Economics of Collective Choice." Buchanan noted in the introduction of the book that "all of the papers [presented at the conference] are devoted to separate aspects of the larger problem of collective decision-making." (1961b: xii) To him, this evidenced that "scholars [we]re now paying increasing attention to the collective decision-making process" (1961b: xi) and that, for this very reason, "Public Finance seem[ed] to be on the threshold of becoming one of the most stimulating fields of inquiry in all of the social science" (xii) – not only in economics.

In 1957, when the program for the conference was drawn up, the economic analysis of collective choices or collective decision-making was not yet a major theme in public finance and was just beginning to attract economists in general.[52]

---

[51] Buchanan to Hoag, December 17, 1956, BP, Hoag, Malcolm, 1954–1968, Box: 52, Folder: 11.

[52] A few years later – in 1959, when the conference took place, or even when the book was published in 1961 – the situation was slightly different. But even then, exceptions were then very rare. Samuelson had given two names, and that was about it. Of course, Musgrave has to be cited for the claims he made in his *The Theory of Public Finance*, but the book would be published in 1959 only.

It is therefore not a surprise that the list of the papers scheduled for a presentation at the conference – a set of, by Buchanan's own admission, "heterogeneous contributions" (xii) – failed to convince the NBER that it was sponsoring a conference in economics. Especially the papers presented during the second day, those with an institutional dimension. The organizing committee was thus obliged to "modif[y] ... the second day's program so as to emphasize the economic content as opposed to the institutional administrative implications which the preliminary proposals carried."[53]

In those years, at least in among the English and American public finance theorists, there was a "tend[ency] to concentrate attention on the impact of the fiscal system on the private market economy. Decisions made by governments have been assumed to be exogenous to the private economic calculus of individuals and firms." (1961b: xi) Fiscal rules are given and the focus is put on the "examination of individual behavior in response to government fiscal action." (1961b: xii) Buchanan was interested in another way of envisaging public finance, one in which "the fiscal system [i]s the means through which individuals make decisions concerning the appropriate amount of resources to be devoted to public rather than to private uses." (1961b: xi) Buchanan was using the conference as an opportunity to develop this new form of political economy and answer Samuelson's suggestion.

Buchanan detailed these elements in the introduction to the volume published in 1961. He signed the text, as it was his and not the organizing committee's viewpoint. It was a programmatic essay on what public finance should be and defined the subject matter. Thus the conference was not just another conference in public finance, but really a step in the building of a new research program – "We need to know much more than we do know about the way in which individuals of a political system organize and finally make collective decisions." (1961b: xiii) These claims were similar to those he made in an application submitted in October 1958—written earlier—to obtain a Ford Foundation Faculty Research Fellowship.

Buchanan contrasted two ways of envisaging public finance. A first approach that consists in studying "the impact of governmental or collective decisions on the behavior of individuals in making private economic decisions." (1958d: 1; emphasis in original) This was not the public finance Buchanan found relevant. He was rather interested in the second, other "important half of public finance of fiscal theory" that had received some attention "in recent years, through the work of Samuelson, Bowen, Musgrave, and a few others" but remained under-developed and "urgently required serious research and study" (1). In this

---

[53] As written in the report the planning committee sent to NBER and that was then sent to the members of the Universities-National Bureau Committee for Economic Research (Carson to the Members, October 31, 1957).

alternative approach, fiscal rules were chosen by the individuals when they decide to act collectively, rather than privately. From this perspective, public finance was viewed as the part of economics that analyzes how individuals choose rules of collective decision-making. Its object was to study:

> the way in which individuals behave in their various capacities as decision-makers for the social group in democratic political organizations. More specifically, the research concentrates on the behavior of individuals in making fiscal decisions, that is, in approving or rejecting tax and expenditure proposals.

Thus, public finance theorists should study the processes through which decisions about how to finance collective needs were made in a democratic system, that is "voting processes, representative assemblies, committees, bureaucracies, and administrative hierarchies." This is what Buchanan planned to do if the application was accepted.

Even if Buchanan had insisted in the past on the rules of the game (1948) or that a pure theory of government finance requires a theory of politics (1949b: 496), he had never really contemplated explicitly the need for economists to study institutions. He did that in the mid to late 1950s. The work and discussions with Vining, and the political situation in the USA and in Virginia in particular, in connection to the massive resistance movement against desegregation played a role in the importance for economists to analyze constitutional rules (see Fleury and Marciano 2018). Yet, it was as a public finance theorist in the context of a re-definition of Public Finance that Buchanan started to apply this new research program. He was now ready to move to the next step. But a new triggering event took place, an intellectual meeting, that led him to write on collective action.

5 Towards a Theory of Collective Action

5.1 Social Imbalance: Another Challenge

If Buchanan's insistence on the need to study the mechanisms through which individuals make collective choices can be traced back to Samuelson, his first analyses were certainly triggered by the publication in May 1958 of *The Affluent Society* (1958), the most successful and controversial book written by Harvard professor of economics John Kenneth Galbraith.[54]

---

[54] The book "sold about 100,000 copies" (Sternsher 1962: 324), "remained . . . onto the best-seller list . . . for twenty-eight weeks" (Heilbroner 1989: 367), and even led to a debate and the use of wealth in the USA, and the need for more public spending (instead of private spending) (see Sternsher 1962: 324–315), a topic of great interest to Buchanan. The success of the book was also beneficial to Galbraith himself – it "made its author, already well known, famous" (Heilbroner

The book was a criticism of the opulence of the American Society.[55] Wealth and opulence were not enough. What was crucial was "'social balance' between the allocation of resources to 'private' goods which can be sold in the market and those 'public' goods which must be provided by political organizations." (Boulding 1959: 81) No society could function properly without such a balance, that was one of the most important claims of *The Affluent Society*, indeed its "main theme" or "thesis" (81). The "disparity between our flow of private and public goods and services," wrote by Galbraith (1958: 252) could only create "an atmosphere of private opulence and public squalor," that would generate "social discomfort and social unhealth" (251), and "social disorder" (259). "Social imbalance," as Galbraith called it, meant violence, pollution, and poverty. And, Galbraith argued, that most Western countries, including the USA, were characterized by such an imbalance. These opulent societies were unhealthily rich for lacking the most basic public goods and services. This was, to Galbraith, "no matter of subjective judgement" (252). The public goods and services that were lacking could be identified and listed, as Galbraith did in his book. Once that was done, government or political action could take place. That was also what Samuelson, Musgrave, and Bator argued. And that was, obviously, the opposite of what Buchanan had written.

As Musgrave, Samuelson, Bator, and many others had argued before Galbraith, government intervention was necessary because individuals could not be trusted to make good decisions. Thus, in contrast to what Buchanan had said, one could not let individuals decide which public goods they wanted provided. Where Galbraith differed from what most economists had written, was in his focus on the limited cognitive capacities of the individuals, rather than on self-interest. This was original and also a particularly controversial claim. To Galbraith, among the three "features of our society" that threatened social balance, "the first of the causes of social imbalance" lied in what he called "the dependence effect" (1958: ch. 11, 152–160).[56] This, rather clearly, meant that consumers could not "make an independent choice between public and private goods" (1958: 260). The "consumers wants" are not "independently determined" (260). They "are created by the process by which they are

---

1989: 367) and can be said to have "played a considerable role in his ascension to the presidency of the *American Economic Association*, and his receipt of the Veblen-Commons Award from the *Association of EvolutionaryEconomics*, and was directly responsible for his receiving the Sidney Hillman Award" (Stanfield 1983: 592).

[55] The idea was not totally new in Galbraith's work. In an essay from 1949, "The American Economy: Substance and Myth," he had noted the contradiction between "a pervasive insecurity" and "actual or realizable well-being" (152). A few years later, his friend Schlesinger had also questioned the opulence of the American society (see Sternsher 1962).

[56] The other two were "the truce on inequality" and "the tendency to inflation."

satisfied" (260), that is by producers through propaganda or advertisement. To Galbraith, consumers are "subject to the forces of advertising and emulation by which production creates its own demand" (260). Therefore, "public services will have an inherent tendency to lag behind" (261). Galbraith writes:

> Advertising operates exclusively, and emulation mainly, on behalf of privately produced goods and services . . . Automobile demand which is expensively synthesized will inevitably have a much larger claim on income than parks or public health or even roads where no such influence operates. The engines of mass communication, in their highest state of development, assail the eyes and ears of the community on behalf of more beverages but not of more schools. (260-261)

Hence, social imbalance characterized American society and created the need for government intervention.

Although he did not then use the expression, Galbraith was "challeng[ing] . . . a major professional truth of economics . . . consumer sovereignty" (2001: 31).[57] Since William H. Hutt – *Economists and the Public* (1936), and to a lesser extent Frederic Benham in *Economics: A General Text-book for Students* (1938), it was admitted that consumers had or should have "the controlling power . . ., in choosing between ends, over the custodians of the community's resources, when the resources by which those ends can be served are scarce" (Hutt 1940: 66). Or, in the more straightforward terms used by Benham, "under capitalism the consumer is king . . . it is the preferences of consumers . . . which determine what shall be produced" (1938: 157). At least, most of the time. Obstacles could prevent consumers from exerting their sovereignty such as monopoly, or, indeed, advertisement and propaganda. But both Hutt and Benham denied that advertisement and propaganda could influence consumers' preferences and determine their wants or choices. The point had been critically noted by Lindley M. Fraser in his reviews of Hutt's *Economists and the Public* and Benham's *Economics: A General Text-book for Students*. Twenty years later, Galbraith gave the criticism a new impetus,

---

[57] Galbraith (1970: 471) would later explain that it was what he had in mind: "The surrender of the sovereignty of the individual to the producer or producing organization is the theme, explicit or implicit, of two books, *The Affluent Society* (2nd ed. rev., Houghton Mifflin Co., 1969) and *The New Industrial State* (Houghton Mifflin Co., 1967)." In *The Essential Galbraith*, a collection of essays obviously devoted to Galbraith, the chapter on the dependence effect was entitled "The Myth of Consumer Sovereignty," which Galbraith presented by saying "My argument in this chapter of *The Affluent Society* was one of the more controversial exercises of my life, for it challenged consumer sovereignty, a major professional truth of economics" (2001: 31). In his review of Galbraith's book, Vining had understood that this was what Galbraith was after. He noted that Galbraith "explains his views regarding how it is that under modern conditions the alleged 'consumer sovereignty' is a delusion" (1959: 117).

putting it back not only at the very heart of the intellectual with his thesis about "social imbalance," but also at the heart of political debate.

Indeed, Galbraith was not just an academic. He had had for some time connections with policy makers. He had worked in Roosevelt's administration during the war, had been one of the founders of *Americans for Democratic Action* – the most important progressive organization in the USA after World War II, with Arthur Schlesinger –, had written columns for *Fortune* and was chairing the *Democratic Advisory Council* to which he belonged since 1958.[58] He had also advised Adlai Stevenson when he ran against Eisenhower in 1956. And, Galbraith's *Affluent Society* is said to have inspired John F. Kennedy during the 1959 presidential campaign that would bring him to the White House.

Buchanan perceived Galbraith, his ideas and influence, as extremely threatening. Galbraith was indeed the "archetype dirigiste in this country" (1963: 13; see also 1962b: 22) Dirigisme, to Buchanan, was the most recent and most dangerous version of socialism. In his view, dirigisme "proposes through wholesale collectivization of human activity, to control or direct the lives of ordinary men towards toward what the advocates believed to be a higher or better society" (1963: 14). Nothing less. The threat posed by such ideas was serious when they were "confined to a few left-wing intellectuals in Cambridge, Massachusetts" (14). They became "deadly serious" when, as Galbraith had done, the "dirigistes" who "hop[ing] to increase their influence, which even today is considerable ... move[d], *en masse*, to Washington and surrounds a sympathetic President" (1963: 14; emphasis in original).

Referring to him and to *The Affluent Society* is certainly not anecdotal in understanding Buchanan's trajectory. In the early 1960s, Buchanan indeed wrote many essays against Galbraith. There were essays written for lectures he delivered, in which he criticized the dirigistes and always mentioned Galbraith, such as "The American Revolution and the Modern Economy" (1962b) or "The Free Society: Fact, Faith, of Fiction" (1963). There were also academic articles in which Buchanan criticized Galbraith. That was the case of "A Note on Public Goods Supply" (1963), co-authored with Milton Kafoglis.

---

[58] A Harvard historian, and a friend of Samuelson's and a friend of Galbraith's too, Schlesinger had pleaded for a "new radicalism," which was a middle of the road form liberalism similar to the one Seymour Harris and Samuelson defended, and which was "morally committed" to "freedom" and "politically committed" to a "limited state" (1949: 150). A limited state that had nonetheless a central role to play. In what was no longer a free market society but rather an administrative one, the rules should be set by the government to avoid that they be set by big firms: "The free market has been increasingly the main theater of economic decisions. We are changing from a market society to an administrative society; and the problem is which set of administrators is to rule ... Big government, for all its dangers, remains democracy's only effective response to big business" (182).

Buchanan and Kafoglis were trying to counter the claim that public goods could not efficiently be provided through a market (or at least a market-like) mechanism because of the externalities in consumption that characterize such goods and that markets fail to take into account. Buchanan and Kafoglis criticized the economists who "us[e] the tools of orthodox welfare analysis" (3) – without naming anyone but referring to "Pigovian welfare economics" in a footnote (6). They also targeted "those who advance the argument concerning the relative 'starvation of the public sector' in America" (3), and here gave two names: Galbraith – *The Affluent Society* – and Francis Bator – who wrote, in the preface of his *The Question of Government Spending. Public Needs and Private Wants*, "we are dangerously shortchanging ourselves on defense, foreign aid, education, urban renewal, and medical services" (1960: xiv; in Buchanan and Kafoglis 1963: 3).[59]

Social imbalance had been on Buchanan's agenda for some time. In 1960, he had thus proposed W. Craig Stubblebine, a student who was at the Thomas Jefferson Center, to write a dissertation that would precisely consist in "evaluat-[ing] critically the social imbalance hypothesis that has been advanced by numerous scientists in the recent years notably by Galbraith" (Buchanan, Thomas Jefferson Center Annual Report, 1960c: 11). Buchanan, as he would explain Stubblebine later, wanted:

> a critical analysis, almost line by line, on the social imbalance argument. I want you to provide the reader with a source that will provide him a handy reference as to what Galbraith, Bator, Lippman, Restion, Dale and the others, including Kennedy in the campaign, have actually said.[60]

An immense and extremely ambitious project indeed, which illustrates Buchanan's concern by the situation. And, while he was working on his dissertation, Stubblebine and Buchanan wrote "Externality" (1962), which can thus be viewed as a part the Buchanan's work against Galbraith and social imbalance.

But the first of Buchanan's criticisms of social imbalance came earlier. It dates from August 1959, shortly after *The Affluent Society* was published. It was then, in all likelihood, that Buchanan wrote "Economic Policy, Free Institutions, and Democratic Process", which he presented at the annual meeting of the Mont-Pelerin Society that took place on September 10 in Oxford (UK). In this

---

[59] Buchanan and Kafoglis also criticized "the dirigistes" for not accepting "the traditional liberal or Western value standards" according to which "[t]he individual is presumed to be the best judge of his own interest so long as his behavior does not affect others significantly" (7).

[60] Buchanan to Stubblebine, May 13, 1962, BP "Externality" drafts and correspondence, 1961–1962, Box: 150, Folder: 2.

article Buchanan, for the first time, proposed a theory of collective action and it was aimed at countering Galbraith's thesis about social imbalance.

5.2 A Theory of Collective Action against Social Imbalance

Buchanan could have criticized Galbraith on various grounds.[61] But in the 1959 essay, in which he first targeted Galbraith, Buchanan focused on majority voting and how collective decisions are made. He insisted that Galbraith's thesis could not hold and that no social imbalance could exist in a democratic society or, to be more precise, a democratic society in which decisions were made by the majority. Although the purpose of the essay was not to refute Galbraith's thesis, that was exactly where his analysis led, namely to:

> an important conclusion which effectively refutes, on purely analytical grounds, the charge advanced by J. K. Galbraith and accepted by many American politicians. Galbraith claims that 'social imbalance' exists today in Western societies because the private sector of the economy has been over-expanded relative to the public sector. It is relatively easy to demonstrate that precisely the opposite tends to be true (13).

The conclusion Buchanan was talking about was that the functioning of modern democracies "leads to an overextension of government activity" (13).

Why? How had Buchanan reached this conclusion? By analyzing how the amount of goods and services produced by the government were decided. This was the starting point and the crucial argument of the essay, that "policy measures emerge from some *collective* decision-making process" (2; emphasis in original). Therefore, before a thesis like Galbraith's could be put forward, one should study how collective decisions were made and look at "the collective choice process" (2). Complementarily, to refute Galbraith's thesis, one should also understand such processes. This meant studying the consequence of the use of majority voting, since in Western democracies, "the most familiar of choosing devices is majority rule" (8) which has been "accept[ed] ... as the 'optimum' means of making collective decisions" (8).

Thus, countering Galbraith was important in Buchanan's choice to analyze the limits of majority voting and to work on collective action. But it was not the only factor that pushed Buchanan in this direction. Among the other elements

---

[61] He could have rejected the dependance effect. He did not, writing just a few words about that. In the introduction of *The Public Finances* (1960), Buchanan insisted on the importance to use the "principle of consumer sovereignty" (1960: 3–4), despite the fact that it ignores the "inconsistency in consumer wants, persuasion by business firms, and the existence of uncertainty" (3) – a sentence that confirms that Buchanan was aware of Galbraith's analysis on this point. The principle was "useful" because it indicates "the goods and services which individuals, expressing their desires as consumers, indicate a willingness and an ability to purchase" (3).

that played a role, one finds the publication, in 1959, of Musgrave's *The Theory of Public Finance. A Study in Public Economy*. Musgrave and Buchanan knew each other. Buchanan also knew of Musgrave's work that he had read since he was writing his dissertation. He felt, and had felt for many years, that Musgrave was envisaging public finance in a way close to his, and close to what Buchanan had in mind when organizing the NBER conference – which consists as said above in viewing public finance in terms of collective choice. And we also know that Buchanan had wanted to write a treatise on public finance since the early 1950s, with a reference to collective action. He had done that with *Public Principles*. Musgrave was also contributing to the same stream of literature – "Within the last decade, the need for developing some theory of collective choice, some pure theory of public finance, has become obvious to many scholars, and important initial advances have been made ... with *The Theory of Public Finance*, Musgrave has written the first English-language treatise in the field" (Buchanan 1960a: 234). And this was an extremely important book – "This book ... should become obligatory reading for all serious students of public finance, and it should remain the standard reference work for graduate study and advanced scholarship for many years" (234).

One of the reasons for which it was an important book was that Musgrave was "grappling with conceptions, issues, and analyses that may ultimately lead to an acceptable theory of collective choice" (234). Musgrave had understood that the satisfaction social wants could not be left to the market because the indivisibility of the benefits received by individuals had to be made through political decisions, and therefore also understood the importance of studying voting rules to allocate resources optimally. However, Musgrave made two mistakes. First, he assumed that there existed a "sharp dividing line between 'social wants' and 'private wants'" (237), that the impossibility to exclude individuals from the consumption of certain goods was a necessary and sufficient condition for collective action. Musgrave was wrong to believe that government intervention was required any time existed a social want – which was identical to what Galbraith was saying. Then, Musgrave defended majority voting. He admitted that it was imperfect, writing "[m]ajority rule is a necessary evil to approximate the desired result, not a principle desired as such" (1959: 14) and that "majority rule does not provide a wholly efficient solution" (126). But he nonetheless concluded that "[t]he result of majority voting is optimal in the sense that it is the solution agreed to by more people than any other" (127) and "the majority solution gives us a welfare maximum of greatest aggregate utility" (127).

Thus, Buchanan chose majority voting as an angle of attack because it would allow him to oppose to both Musgrave and his approach of public finance, and to Galbraith and social imbalance. But one element of the jigsaw was still missing, the element that would allow Buchanan to indeed explain why majority voting cannot lead to social imbalance. He had already written on majority voting in his dissertation (1948), in his 1954 review of Kenneth Arrow's book (1951), and, again, around the summer of 1958, in "Positive Economics, Welfare Economics and Political Economy" (1959). It was Tullock, who was instrumental in allowing Buchanan to transform his ideas into a weapon against Galbraith.

In August 1959 Buchanan and Tullock started working together, even if it was not on a common project. Tullock was at UVA on a fellowship that Buchanan and Nutter had granted him, after they had met at the 1957 annual conference of the *American Economic Association* in Philadelphia. Tullock was developing a general theory of politics, which partly consisted in criticizing the majority rule. During the first half of 1959, Tullock had written "Democratic Marginalism" (1959a), which he expanded in "Problems of Majority Voting" (1959b), published in the June issue of the *Journal of Political Economy*.[62] Tullock's conclusion was that "the system of majority voting is not by any means an optimal method of allocating resources" (1959b: 579). It allowed and even incited individuals or groups of individuals to form coalitions that would therefore force the rest of the population to accept what they want and also to pay for it.

Buchanan encouraged Tullock to continue this line of inquiry, commenting extensively on *A Preliminary Investigation of the Theory of Constitutions*, the eighty-five-page long monograph Tullock had produced compiling four of his essays including "Problems in Majority Voting" and a chapter entitled "External Costs" that became the sixth chapter of *The Calculus of Consent* (1962).[63] And, in August 1959, Buchanan even wrote his own version of the limits of majority voting, "Simple Majority Voting, Game Theory, and Resource Use" (1961a).[64]

Buchanan demonstrated, as Tullock had, that majority voting gave minority groups the possibility to buy the votes of other minority groups and form coalitions capable of implementing public projects that would benefit only their members while being financed by the entire population. Some of the conclusions one could derive from this demonstration had already been drawn by Tullock, such as the injustice that came with spreading of the costs on the entire population and limiting the benefits to a part of it. Buchanan spoke of the

---

[62] "Democratic Marginalism" is an undated ten-page manuscript. Tullock's correspondence, in particular with Buchanan, indicates that it was written at the end of 1958 or the beginning of 1959.

[63] The comments were so abundant that Tullock wrote that Buchanan "should not only receive credit for what merits the monograph has, but also bear fair share of any criticisms which it may arouse" (1959b: i).

[64] The paper was submitted on August 24, 1960, that is, when Buchanan and Tullock were revising *The Calculus of Consent*.

"exploitation" of the minority by the majority and the inefficiency of the process: Buchanan demonstrated that, under certain conditions, "socially undesirable" or "wasteful" projects would be adopted – or that "there exists nothing in the operation of majority voting to direct funds to the most productive employments" (345) or "there is nothing in the operation of the majority-rule device that will act to prevent socially undesirable projects from securing adoption" (344). And, as a corollary, Buchanan made a point that was not explicit in Tullock, "there will be a tendency for the public sector to be over-extended, relatively" (344; see also 347). He repeated this conclusion four times; a conclusion that was the opposite of what Galbraith was claiming.

Buchanan completed his refutation of Galbraith's claims by adding another argument on "fiscal illusion", the only cognitive limitation Buchanan admitted. Buchanan had discovered the concept when he was in Italy, having read Amilcare Puviani's *Teoria della Illusione Finanziaria* (*Theory of Fiscal Illusion* 1903) and Mauro Fasiani's *Principii delle Scienze delle Finanze* (*Principles of Public Finance* 1950). But he did not know much of the concept yet, as evidenced by the mention made, once in passing, in *Public Principles* (1958e: 120), and by the few pages devoted to the concept in the survey on "The Italian Tradition in Fiscal Theory," written in 1958 and published in *Fiscal Theory and Political Economy* (1960b). Buchanan nonetheless knew enough of it to understand that fiscal illusion prevented individuals to perceive the costs of the projects they were asked to vote for, and more precisely to underestimate them. The consequence was clear: Individuals who were victims of fiscal illusion would therefore accept more projects than in the absence of fiscal illusion. The overextension of the public section would be amplified:

> The distortions become more pronounced when we allow for some ignorance on the part of these participants. If the institutional structure is such that the real costs of policy measures tend to be concealed, the beneficiary groups will find it easier to secure the necessary allies in support of any particular (15)

Thus, "two factors ... majority voting and the fiscal illusion are, therefore, mutually reinforcing rather than offsetting. Both tend to force the public sector to expand relative to the private sector." (16) Put differently, both factors prevent the social imbalance Galbraith had diagnosed.

5.3 A Defense of Unanimity

If acting against a (nonexistent) social imbalance was not necessary, it was nonetheless necessary to act against the contrary tendency, the "over-expan [sion] of the public sector" (17). This could mean "dispelling" (17) fiscal illusion, which could be done by improving the level of information available to taxpayers or by linking the tax and spending sides of the budget. But this would not suffice, "a more fundamental reform is needed," Buchanan claimed (17–18). The overexpansion of the public sector was mainly caused by majority voting, and according to Buchanan, this was what should be targeted.

The result could be achieved through "a genuine moral regeneration of the politician, the legislator. If politicians could be convinced that they have a solemn duty and obligation to act on a Kantian plane of objectivity and impartiality, substantial improvement might be made" (18). For Buchanan, such a reform "requires a greater faith in human nature than many of us possess. The frailty of human psychology might not be able to withstand the intense conflict of loyalties that such a role would inflict on the individual legislator" (18). Rather than changing individuals, one should take them as they are and change the institutions in which they make decisions. Thus, the solution could only consist in "trying to secure certain changes in the political constitution" (18). This meant "remov[ing] . . . certain important decisions from majority-vote determination, as Wicksell so acutely and clearly recognized long ago. For such issues, some shift in the direction of greater consensus seems to be essential" (18). In Buchanan's view, this meant unanimity.

It would guarantee that no one would be harmed by collective action and guarantee Pareto optimal decisions. Buchanan repeated the crucial point he had already made: The "unanimity rule is the political prototype of the Pareto rule for determining whether or not changes are desirable, a parallel which Knut Wicksell recognized even before Pareto" (4). But unanimity did not mean that all would benefit from the collective decisions made. That was impossible. Some would win, some would lose. That was why unanimity could not be used without a "full compensation" of the losers by the winners, as could be found in the works of Kaldor, Hicks, and Scitovsky. Therefore, some would directly benefit from the collective action and others would benefit indirectly. Unanimity was guaranteed. Here, too, Buchanan repeated what he had written in "Positive Economics" – "Full compensation is essential . . . in order to decide which one from among the many possible social policy changes does, in fact, satisfy the genuine Pareto rule" (1959: 129).

Which did not mean that the rule was easy and cheap to implement. Buchanan was aware of "[t]he immensity of the practical difficulties" (7) there were if such a rule to make decisions was used. But, as he had said many times, that was "no argument against the conceptual validity of the principle." Unanimity should be the norm. Deviations were possible in very specific cases only, as if the cost of achieving a unanimous consent were "out of the line with the importance of the issues" (7).

Historically, "Economic Policy, Free Institutions, and Democratic Process" with its sketch of an "economic theory . . . of democratic decision-making" (3), or, paraphrasing Tullock, of an "Economic Theory of Constitutions" (7–8), reads like a twenty-page summary of *The Calculus of Consent* (1962) written before Buchanan and Tullock had even decided to work together. It was indeed in September 1959 that the decision was made to "collaborate on a joint project" Buchanan and Tullock (1962: xix). A project on which they presumably began work in January 1960, after Buchanan had sent *The Public Finances* (1960d) to the publisher. Therefore, *The Calculus* is as much a response to Samuelson, Musgrave, and other welfare economists as it is to Galbraith and the "social imbalancers." In the book, as in his subsequent articles, Buchanan added other elements that complement his views on collective action, explaining why and when collective action should take place, and what forms it should take.

6 A Theory of Collective Action

6.1 Irrelevant Externalities and Opportunity Costs

To define the boundaries of collective action two lines need to be drawn. The first is between private and collective action. The first step in establishing a theory of collective action consists in explaining when individuals need or wish to resort to collective action. In this matter, Buchanan's views were extremely different from those of the social imbalancers and from those of the "old" welfare economists. Both categories of thinkers believed that there exists a dividing line between what market mechanisms can do and what political or governmental institutions must do. Moreover, such line is given by some objective characteristics: The interdependence between utility and production functions, the existence of indivisibilities, the impossibility to exclude consumers from the benefits generated by the provision of the good, and the existence of a need. They similarly "confused" the "mere presence of public or collective needs . . . with the necessity for satisfying them" (1957: 175).

Buchanan disagreed. He did not deny the existence of needs, including "[t]he need for more and better highway facilities, for more schoolrooms, for more slum clearance, etc., may be readily admitted" (175). No more than he denied that interdependencies or indivisibilities and the impossibility to exclude potential consumers can exist objectively. He denied that these objective problems had to lead mechanically to an action to deal with them. He wrote, as early as in 1957, that "[t]he existence of 'undeniable' need does nothing toward proving that action must be taken to meet it" (175). With the more specific words of public economics, those words Musgrave had used in his 1959 book, "the impossibility of exclusion is not a necessary condition for collective action in satisfying a genuinely 'social want'" (1960: 237). Or, as he and Tullock wrote in *The Calculus*: "*The existence of external effects of private behavior is neither a necessary nor a sufficient condition for an activity to be placed in the realm of collective choice*" (1962: 61; emphasis in original). To Buchanan, there were many problems that individuals could not solve privately but that did not warrant collective action.

To understand what Buchanan meant, let us examine some of the examples one finds in his work. For instance, when Tiebout argued that zoning laws could be used to exclude potential users from the consumption of the public good they did not have paid for (1961: 94; see also Tiebout 1956: 420), Buchanan replied that, even if "[p]rohibition on entry" (1961b: 129) could achieve that goal, it is not what matters. Creating these exclusions has a cost: to exclude potential free riders the contributors would be forced to "forego capital gains in order to prevent the entry of 'undesirables' into the community" (128). Costs might be too large compared to the benefits – "this sacrifice of capital gains on possible land holdings may be more than offset by the retention of a greater share of taxpayers' surplus" (128). If that was the case, it was not rational to create such devices to engage in collective action against the free riders.

Another example is "[t]he color of the automobile that your colleague drives" which "certainly influences your own utility to some extent" (Buchanan and Tullock 1962: 52). In that case, there exists an externality – "Spillover effects are clearly present" – but this does not mean that something should be done – "you will probably prefer to allow your colleague free individual choice as regards this class of decisions." This externality is said to be "negligible" (Buchanan 1960a: 237) or "Pareto irrelevant" as Buchanan and Stubblebine wrote (1962). Relevance (or irrelevance) took two forms. It had first to do with a "desire" – "to modify the behaviour of another" (374) – and then, second, the "ability" to do so. No gains should be expected from its removal.[65] Obviously, acting collectively to control the color of the private cars would be too costly compared to the benefits that could be obtained.

From these examples, one understands Buchanan's point: needs "are always relative, never absolute" (1957: 175; see 1958f: 77). They do not exist object-ively – "we tend to accept presumably objective standards of need which do not exist." (1958f: 78) and "there is no objective standard to be utilized at this point" (1957: 175). Needs are relative because they exist only in reference to their cost.

---

[65] Buchanan and Stubblebine defined relevance in two ways. First, an externality is "potentially relevant when the activity, to the extent that it is actually performed, generates any desire on the part of the externally benefited (damaged) party (A) to modify the behaviour of the party empowered to take action (B) through trade, persuasion, compromise, agreement, convention, collective action, etc." (373–374). Second, an externality is "Pareto-relevant when the extent of the activity may be modified in such a way that the externally affected party, A, can be made better off without the acting party, B, being made worse off." (374).

Thus, in the words Buchanan used when he wrote to the editor of the *New York Times* in May 1957 to comment an editorial entitled "Taxpayers Oppose Taxes," one cannot assume that existing "over-riding need[s]" would "somehow [be] divorced from cost considerations."[66]

That needs are relative and that their satisfaction depends on their costs come from the fact that many needs have always to be satisfied at the same time and that, consequently, a choice has to be made between them. Choosing to satisfy one need meant not satisfying another one, rather it meant sacrificing other needs. Put differently, the problem of satisfying some needs, or to spend public money, should be discussed in terms of opportunity costs.

Buchanan was clear that the "concept of alternative or opportunity cost" was "the central principle of economics" and "that we stand always in danger of overlooking it, especially in discussions of public policy issues" (1957: 175). He insisted: "Paralleling each additional need or desire, be it public or private, there is some cost of meeting it, a cost which can be measured in terms of the goods and services sacrificed or given up." (175). Or, public goods, such as "schools must be paid for in terms of goods and services which taxpayers must forego, now or later."[67] Therefore, as he said to the subcommittee on Fiscal Policy of the Joint Economic Committee before which he appeared at the end of 1957, "We satisfy one need, be it public or private, only through forgoing the satisfaction of another." (1958f: 78). In the extended version of his statement, he wrote: "We can collectively satisfy the need for more school rooms only by giving up something else – dwelling units, automobiles, or what have you." (1957: 175).

6.2 Who Knows the Opportunity Costs?

To use opportunity costs to draw the line between private and collective action, and delineate the domain of collective action, is crucial. Indeed, only those who pay for, and benefit from, public goods and services – that is, the taxpayers – are able to know what they sacrifice (or gain) by choosing one public good or service instead of another. Why? The answer was in the above mentioned letter Buchanan sent Samuelson in which he explained that individual preferences are revealed by their choices.[68] Only the individuals have access to their preferences. He made the point again, and more explicitly, in "Positive Economics, Welfare Economics and Political Economy" (1959) or in the preliminary version of the article, entitled "Ignorance, Ethics and Political Economy" (1958b). "Utility remains *subjective*" (1958b: 6; emphasis in original) Buchanan wrote, before changing it to utility "is a *subjectively* quantifiable

---

[66] Buchanan to the editor, *The New York Times*, May 20, 1957. [67] Ibid.
[68] Buchanan to Samuelson, February 25, 1955.

magnitude" (1959: 126; emphasis in original). This means that, "[i]f "utility" exists at all, it is quantifiable only to the individual" (1958b: 8). Thus, the individual preferences, the "ranking of alternatives" remain concealed "until and unless that ranking is revealed by the overt action of the individual in choosing among alternatives" (8). Therefore, because of the subjectivity of individual preferences, "[o]nly those directly responsible for decisions can strike a final balance on the basis of their own attempts at measurement" (1957: 179). The notions of subjective and objective costs will become very important in Buchanan's work, analyzed in details in *Cost and Choice* (1969), was already there ten years earlier.

That individual preferences are known only to individuals themselves means that they cannot be known to any outside observer, for whom, wrote Buchanan, they "must remain forever concealed" (8). Not *forever* actually, Buchanan wrote: "[t]he economist can say, *ex post*, that the individual prefers A to B because he has *chosen* A over B. *Ex ante*, the economist can say nothing all" (8; emphasis in original). Thus, until and unless the individual choice has revealed them, the economist, "must remain fundamentally ignorant concerning the actual ranking of alternatives" (1958b: 8; 1959: 126). Assuming that one could be sufficiently "omniscient" to be "able to 'read' individual preference functions" (126) and thus to determine a priori which needs should be satisfied and how much public goods should be financed, would be a mistake. Therefore, only the taxpayers should decide whether or not they want to spend public resources and satisfy a need directly or indirectly. As Buchanan wrote, "[i]n a democratic society, the genuine collective needs of the people are expressed only through their actions as voters, pressure-group members, legislators, and administrators" (1957: 175). Indivisibilities and interdependencies are problematic and have to be dealt with if and only if individuals voluntarily decide to act collectively against them – "Public needs become objectively meaningful only when people indicate a willingness to bear the necessary costs" (175). Observing, as external observers such as economists could do, the existence of interdependencies did not mechanically imply that something should be done to remove them. The only rule to decide whether or not a good should be produced remained the "individual evaluations" (Buchanan 1960a: 237).

Certainly, Buchanan admitted, "the values of taxpayers indicated by their choices of automobiles (or other private goods) over school buildings may be criticized and deplored."[69] He also agreed that the choices made by the individuals might not please the economists or the decision-makers. However, he refused to assume "better" decisions than the one made by taxpayers were

---

[69] Buchanan to the editor, *The New York Times*, May 20, 1957.

possible. Such an assumption mistakenly "suggests that there exists some objective means of determining when a school building adds more to the general welfare than does a fleet of new automobiles."[70] This is not the case. Buchanan was clear about that – "It is generally admitted that such objective measures cannot, by their very nature, be constructed." Therefore, economists or decision-makers should not try to alter individual preferences. They should not try to impose their preferences on the individuals. They should remain positive in their approach and not become normative. This meant informing citizens and taxpayers of the possible consequences of their choices and decisions but leave them "free to choose" (Buchanan 1954c: 120) what they want. Buchanan defined freedom as the "absence of coercion" (1954d: 340).

Therefore, instead of defining categories of goods – private and public or social and even merit – Buchanan suggested to distinguish modes of provision of goods: the "private market action" and "collective action" (1960a). Later (1965b: 11), he would be more explicit:

> Public finance theorists have, by and large, accepted the classification between 'private goods,' which may be efficiently supplied through market institutions, and 'public goods,' which cannot be so supplied, as being determined by forces not subject to social control. Closer examination reveals, however, that this important dividing line may itself be variable.

6.3 The Forms of Collective Action

After individuals have decided that a good should be produced collectively, the next and second step consists in asking which forms collective action should take. In particular, in asking if collective action necessarily means government intervention. In those years, there was a relative consensus around a positive answer to this question: If markets failed, it was to governments to act. Thus, not only was it believed that the identification of a problem mechanically meant acting to remove it, but also that the action had to be political and had to involve the government.[71]

That was Galbraith's view, as said in Section 5.1. Musgrave's too, who was convinced that when it comes to "social wants," "[t]he exclusion principle cannot be applied," which means that "[t]he single individual's share in the benefits received from the services cannot be isolated or separated from the

---

[70] Buchanan to the editor, *The New York Times*, May 20, 1957.

[71] Reviewing *The Calculus*, James Meade (1963: 101) noted that "in discussing external economies and diseconomies economists have been much too ready to call in the State as a *deus ex machina* to remove the imperfections of the laissez-faire market without examining the implications of this view for the political, as contrasted with the economic, behaviour of the individual citizen."

benefits received by other individuals," and that therefore "[t]he inapplicability of the exclusion principle . . . makes collective or governmental action necessary" (Buchanan 1960a: 235). Or, more broadly, it was what Pigovian economists believed, those who derive from the "basic Pigovian theorem" (Buchanan 1962a: 17) – according to which "[t]he market 'fails' to the extent that there exist divergencies between marginal private products and marginal social products and/or between marginal private costs and marginal social costs"(17) – a normative conclusion for whom, the "observation that there exist divergencies between marginal private products and marginal social products and/or between marginal private costs and marginal social costs" necessarily implied that the divergence should be "reduced or eliminated by the shift of an activity from market to political organisation" (17). Indeed, as Stubblebine would stress in a letter to Buchanan about his dissertation, one of the "points which form the core of the [social imbalance] hypothesis . . . [is] . . . the standard externality argument," according to which "all activities characterized by externalities (but more specifically, external economics) call for government financing and operation."[72]

And, again, Buchanan disagreed. As he and Stubblebine would write, "[t]here is not a *prima facie* case for intervention in all cases where an externality is observed to exist" (1962: 381). Collective action need not be political (and coercive). It could also be private (and voluntary). Thus, and that was indeed one important innovation Buchanan and Tullock introduced in *The Calculus*, and a major difference with the "dirigistes," between private and "political" collective action, with government intervention and the collectivization of activities, there was room for "voluntary co-operative" and "contractual" arrangements (Buchanan and Tullock 1962: 46).

Choosing between one form or the other depended on the respective costs of each mode of organization. When the costs of dealing with problems through political collective action were higher than the costs of devising private contractual arrangements, then no government intervention was required, "beyond," obviously, "the initial minimal delineation of the power of individual disposition over resources" (45). Voluntary co-operative arrangements were sufficient. Then, when the costs of government intervention were lower than the costs of private collective action, and in that case only, political collective action was required. In other words, government intervention was not related to the existence of interdependencies, indivisibilities, or any objective characteristics. It could therefore be decided in advance. It could only be chosen ex-post, because of the failure or incapacity to organize collective action privately. When

---

[72] Stubblebine to Buchanan, April 27, 1962, BP "Externality" drafts and correspondence, 1961–1962, Box: 150, Folder: 2.

and if individuals were not able to organize themselves collectively, then, they would delegate the task to a third party, to the government.

In addition, and this was a point of the utmost importance, Buchanan and Tullock also showed that there were conditions in which no constitutional provision was required: "If property rights are carefully defined" or "[a]fter human and property rights are initially defined," which meant that "the costs of organizing decisions voluntarily should be zero," then "*all* externalities would be eliminated by voluntary private behavior of individuals regardless of the initial structure of property rights" (48; emphasis in original). They insisted:

> [i]f the decision-making costs are absent . . . "[a]ll externalities, negative and positive, will be eliminated as a result of purely voluntary arrangements that will be readily negotiated among private people. (62)

> in the absence of costs of organizing decision-making, voluntary arrangements would tend to be worked out which would effectively remove all relevant externalities. (89)

> if we disregard the costs of making the required arrangements, voluntary action would more or less automatically take place that would be sufficient to "internalize" all externality, that is, to reduce expected external costs to zero. (90)

The repetition and insistence is directly linked to the importance of the result, which meant that one could trust individuals to find solutions to the problems they face. In other words, after having demonstrated that the existence of a problem or of a need did not mean that something should be done about it, Buchanan was making a second point: What should be done does not necessarily mean government intervention.

Buchanan and Tullock may also have insisted because they were aware of the similarity of their conclusion Coase was reaching in "The Problem of Social Cost" (1960). Since April 1960, Buchanan knew that Coase had presented a paper on "the externality problem and on the television 'payola'" at the University of Chicago and at the Virginia economic club, where his ideas had raised an "enormous amount of polemic."[73] In August, he wrote to Otto Davis that Coase's work was important:

---

[73] Francesco Forte, who was at UVA invited by Buchanan who was actually in London, had written Buchanan in April: "Coase made two successful speeches in Chicago on the externality problem and on the television "payola." Also at the Virginia economic club he made a speech on externality. There was an enormous amount of polemic . . . In Chicago, as he told me, he changed the direction of his criticism, arguing that the Pigovian argument is wrong. Seems that the public was well impressed." (Forte to Buchanan, April 22, 1960, BP, Forte, Francesco, circa 1960s, Box: 47, Folder: 5.)

Ronald Coase is doing some very interesting work in this aspect of welfare economics. He argues, quite convincingly, that there will be no difference in resource allocation whether or not externalities exist, provided that the market functions perfectly (in our terminology, if decision-costs are zero). So he is very close to our side in this matter, and most of economic theory has been wrong on it since Pigou, I now think.[74]

Buchanan and Tullock, and Coase and Davis – in an article with Andrew Whinston, "Externalities, Welfare, and the Theory of Games" (1962) – had made the same point, that "[t]he divergence between social and marginal products employed as a criterion for social policy changes has been shown to represent no criterion at all" (1960c: 2). Buchanan noted that in the 1960 report about the activity of the Thomas Jefferson Center. To evidence the consistency of their research program was important since the Center was still young, and also because it was criticized for being ideologically oriented (see Medema 2009; Levy and Peart 2020).

6.4 Why Politics Is *Not* More Efficient Than Markets

Government intervention in the presence of externalities could be justified, and preferred to private collective action, if it were more efficient. Was it? Buchanan answered in the negative in "Politics, Policy and the Pigovian Margins," published in 1962 but written in 1960 when Buchanan was at the *London School of Economics* and just after a first draft of *The Calculus* had been completed. The article belongs to the body of work Buchanan developed to refute the theses of Samuelson, Musgrave, Galbraith, and other social imbalancers.

The reference to Pigou was new to Buchanan, who had rarely and not particularly critically referred to Pigou in his work prior to 1960.[75] But it made sense after Coase and after Davis and Whinston that Buchanan should formulate his ideas in the terms of an opposition to Pigou. Ideas that themselves were not new. The arguments Buchanan used can indeed be traced back to "Individual Choice in Voting and the Market" (1954b), which he adapted to the externality problem. As in his previous article, and as he had written in *The Calculus* and in "Simple Majority Voting, Game Theory and Resource Use," Buchanan compared two "extreme and contrasting" models of human behavior.

---

[74] Buchanan to Davis, August 16, 1960, BP.

[75] He cited *A Study in Public Finance* (1929) superficially – except *in Public Principles of Public Debt* (1958) – and *Wealth and Welfare* (1912) and *The Economics of Welfare* (1920) were mentioned only in "The Road Case Re-examined" (1956). Even then, Buchanan had not been critical of Pigou. And, Buchanan had never referred to Pigou in his rather frequent attacks against the externality argument (1957, 1959; or in *The Calculus*).

At one end, the standard economic representation of man according to which rational and self-interested individuals make decisions by comparing marginal costs and benefits and for whom "[n]o considerations of the 'public' or the 'social' interest are assumed to enter this . . . calculus" (1962a: 20). These individuals are, in other words, narrowly self-interested. And, at the other end of the behavioral spectrum, the model that assumes that "each individual . . . tries to identify himself with the community of which he is a member and . . . tries to act in the genuine interest of the whole group" (22). Those individuals, Buchanan wrote using the reference he had started to use in *The Calculus* and that would become more frequent in the next decade, following a "Kantian-like rule of action" (22).

Then, what would be the respective performances of two institutional mechanisms that could be used to deal with externalities, markets (private action), and politics (collective action) under these assumptions? That was, Buchanan wrote, "intuitively clear" (20, 22). If individuals were self-interested, external diseconomies were unavoidable and markets failed to allocate resources efficiently. Private and social marginal costs would diverge. The narrowly self-interested could not be expected to adopt prosocial behaviors and take into account the consequences of their actions on others. But politics would not be more efficient. The problem would not be dealt with if the activity generating the external effect was collectivized. More precisely, it would not work if the decision was made by the majority. Here, Buchanan repeated the point he and Tullock had made. Indeed, if one assumes that individuals are rational and self-interested when they vote, that is if one extends "the behavioural assumptions of orthodox economic theory . . . to political choice-making" (20), then one can predict that individuals would vote "to advance [their] own interest" (20). They would form coalitions to obtain gains that would be "shared symmetrically (equally) among all members of the dominant coalition" (20) but "secured . . . at the expense of the other members of the political group" (20). Therefore, the private benefits of the individuals belonging to the dominant coalitions would be larger than the benefits of the rest of the population, or that the private cost they have to pay would be smaller than the social cost. Thus, politics with majority rule and rational voters give the same result as markets: "Externalities must be present in any solution reached by the voting process under all less-than-unanimity rules." (21)

Alternatively, if individuals were all following Kantian rules of action, the political process would not fail and would not lead to the collectivization of activities creating a gap between private and social costs that need not to be collectivized. Indeed, since each individual "acts on the basis of identifying his own interest with that of the larger group," no one would try to vote for a proposition that consists in shifting the costs to the minority. Indeed, wrote Buchanan, "no deliberate exploitation of minority by majority can take place through the political process regardless of the voting rule that is applied" (23). That was the point about the decisions made by Kantian farmers (Tullock 1959b; Buchanan and Tullock 1962; Buchanan 1961a). So the Pigovians were right, but to a certain extent only. If individuals were behaving as Kantians, politics would not fail but then markets would not fail either. The Kantian would also "try to identify himself with the group as a whole and to act in accordance with what he considers to be the 'public' interest" (23). Individuals would take into account the consequences of their actions on others or, put differently, reason in terms of marginal social instead of private cost. External effects would be removed. Thus, Buchanan concluded, "[t]he Pigovian divergence between marginal private product and marginal social product disappears in both the market and the political organization of activity in this universal benevolence model" (23).

The main conclusion was clear: Politics was as flawed as markets or markets were as efficient as collective action. What Pigovian economists claimed, namely that politics could solve problems that markets could not, was valid only if individuals acted as Kantian in politics and were self-interested on markets, that is only "under the assumption that individuals respond to different motives when they participate in market and in political activity" (23). Or, still in other words, it was valid within the "behavioural model . . . which has been called 'the bifurcated man'" (23).

To Buchanan, this assumption of a "behavioral dichotomy" (24) was "clearly extreme" (24) and "naive" (25). It was preferable to work by assuming a "behavioural consistency": If individuals were supposed to be self-interested on markets, then they should also be supposed to be self-interested in their political decisions; reciprocally, if individuals were supposed "to identify [themselves] with the group as a whole," the same assumption should be used to analyze economic decisions and political choices. Motives of action do not change when the institutional structure changes, as the Pigovian assumed, although behaviors may change. Thus, an individual could behave "socially" (24) in politics, if he "is made fully conscious of the fact that he is choosing *for* the whole group" (24; emphasis in original) but this did not mean that he was no longer self-interested. Consistency in motives had to be maintained. Buchanan believed that self-interest was the most fruitful of the two models. Under this assumption, the claim that externalities could be dealt with through political processes did not hold.

Or, in a last attempt at rescuing it, Buchanan wrote that Pigou's claim might be valid for pure public goods if each individual was "required [to vote] by includ[ing] in his calculus a share of the total marginal cost . . . that is proportional to his individualised share of the total marginal benefits" (26). This meant that taxes could vary from one individual to the other, but all would "pay for the marginal unit of the collective good or service in proportion to the marginal benefit enjoyed" (26). Thus, Buchanan was saying, that the Pigovian inference about the collectivization of externalities could be valid if a means was found to individualize prices for public goods. That was a repetition of the same old claim about individualized prices. However, Buchanan did not believe that it would work. Such a cost-sharing mechanism, he wrote, was "politically unimaginable" (27), "conceptually impossible" (27), and therefore "of little practical value" (28). Therefore, no realistic institutional mechanism existed that could prevent the members of the majority to oblige the members of the minority to pay more than their share of the total marginal costs. Or, put differently, as long as prices could not be individualized, the collectivization of activities generating externalities could not be defended as a general and systematic principle.

6.5 The Conditions for Cooperation

6.5.1 Size and Cooperation

Voluntary collective action, based on unanimous consent and therefore on individualized prices for public goods (without which no consensus would be possible), requires important behavioral assumptions, that individuals reveal their true preferences and do not adopt "antisocial" or "unreasonable" behaviors (1959: 135). To behave antisocially or unreasonably meant to refuse to cooperate even though it appears clearly that cooperation would be Pareto improving. That is even though the unreasonable individuals would benefit from this collective action. Put differently, unreasonable and antisocial behaviors corresponded to what Musgrave or Samuelson tended to see as normal and the main reason for which they claimed that coercion was necessary. And Buchanan agreed with that – "Insofar as 'antisocial' or unreasonable individuals are members of the group, consensus, even where genuine 'mutual gains' might be present, may be impossible." (135). But he disagreed on the fact that individuals would behave unreasonably.

One remembers Buchanan's early conviction that the voluntary exchange theory was valid and that individuals would pay for the public goods they consume, for the external effects their actions generate, as they do for private goods. In the early 1960s, he had not changed his mind. In "What Should Economists Do?", the presidential address he delivered at the 1963 annual meetings of the *Southern Economic Association,* Buchanan again insisted on the individuals' willingness to cooperate with others. This was a fact:

"Individuals are observed to cooperate with one another, to reach agreements, to trade" (1964b: 219). This was explained by the benefits individuals gain from trading with others: "The motivation for individuals to engage in trade, the source of the propensity, is surely that of 'efficiency,' defined in the personal sense of moving from less preferred to more preferred positions, and doing so under mutually acceptable terms" (219). To Buchanan, cooperation based on self-interest was a normal way of behaving. Rather than free-riding that appeared to be so crucial to Musgrave or Samuelson. Buchanan, who used the term for the first time, spoke of the "spectre of the 'free rider' found in many shapes and forms in the literature of modern public finance theory" (220). As if the behavior was pathological.

These individuals could be assumed to be reasonable because many of them most of the time behave reasonably, which had a consequence on what economists did and should do. Rather than trying to identify the situations in which individuals will try to free ride and studying the means that could be used to force them to cooperate, the role of the economist was precisely to understand the conditions under which individuals voluntarily act collectively to solve or prevent market failures without having to rely on government intervention. Economists must "concentrate their attention on a particular form of human activity and upon the various institutional arrangements that arise as a result of this form of activity" (Buchanan 1964b: 213–214). This was the research program Buchanan outlined in "What Should Economists Do?," and on which he had already started to work for a few years. This work had allowed Buchanan to identify the role of a crucial factor, the number of persons involved in the problem.

Let us note here that the public finance theorists that Buchanan had found so interesting when he had written his dissertation were themselves aware that numbers matter. One of the economists Buchanan referred in his dissertation, who was one of the rare among English-speaking economists to write on the Italian public finance theorists, Frederic Benham, explained that the form collective action would take depended on the number of individuals wishing to organize a collective action. Benham had written that, if a "fairly small number of men ... [with ...] equal incomes and tastes" (1934b: 451) desire to provide goods and services collectively, they can "form clubs and similar associations" (451). He viewed clubs as groups of individuals who decide "to spend part of their incomes upon the collective provision of certain services" (451). Having identical tastes and incomes, individuals would receive the same benefits from the use of the good and then would pay the same tax – "all would contribute equally, for incomes and tastes would be equal" (452). All would also contribute "voluntarily" (452) under a crucial condition: "provided the others also agreed" (452). But, if the group is no longer homogenous – Benham did not refer to larger groups – because individuals have different incomes and tastes, "including those arising from their different locations or occupations" (453), then decisions on "expenditures and contributions" (453) must be made by voting. To guarantee neutral taxation, the only satisfactory solution was to choose the program that "would meet with unanimous agreement" (453).

How much, and if Buchanan was influenced by Benham is hard to tell. It nonetheless remains that his explanation of the existence of states was close to the theory Buchanan started to develop in the late 1950s.[76] The first time Buchanan stressed that voluntary collective action could fail "when the interactions extend over a large number of persons" was in "Simple Majority Voting, Game Theory and Resource Use". One remembers that Buchanan wrote the paper during the summer of 1959 as a complement to Tullock's "Problems of Majority Voting".

In his analysis of how farmers were willing to vote to repair roads, Tullock had introduced a distinction between two types of individuals that Buchanan will use again many times afterwards. There were the Kantians, on one hand, that is, those who "vote to repair a given road in the same way as he would vote for repairs his own road" (1959b: 573). And, on the other hand, the maximizers who "vot[e] against all proposals to repair roads other than his own and voting for proposals to repair his road at every opportunity" (574).

Then, the question was: Would individuals behave as Kantians, or as maximizers? Tullock explained that "any individual farmer" has an interest in behaving as a maximizer if he expects others to behave as Kantians. That is, he has an interest in voting only in favor of proposals to repair his own road and against the proposals aimed at repairing the roads used by other famers. Indeed, "his taxes would be reduced or his road kept in better-than-average repair" (574). If other farmers imitate him, this would increase the standard of repair on the roads owned by the maximizers, and decrease the standard of repair on others' roads while reducing their share of the costs and increasing the costs incurred by other taxpayers (574).

Thus, the general level of repair of the roads would be lower in a community in which individuals behave as maximizers rather than as Kantians. And that would be at the advantage of maximizers and at the disadvantage of Kantians since the latter support the cost of repair of the roads of the maximizers who, by contrast, only pay for the repair of their own roads or those of the members of

---

[76] For details on Benham and Buchanan, see Marciano (2018).

their coalition. Consequently, Kantians, obviously "exploited by the maximizers" (1959b: 574) or put differently, realizing that "virtue . . . conspicuously is not paying" (575), would become "tired" (574) of "never hav[ing] [their] own road repaired [while] pay[ing] heavy taxes for the support of repair jobs on other roads" (576). They would eventually "switch to a maximizing pattern of behavior" (574). Actually, there exists a threshold in the number of maximizers within the group of farmers under which Kantians accept to be exploited. Kantians could tolerate a certain number of maximizers in the community before departing from the moral rule of conduct themselves. When the proportion of maximizers becomes too important, Kantians too change their behavior and become maximizers.

Buchanan's own article extended and deepened Tullock's.[77] Starting with the same problem – farmers and road repair – he discussed how collective decisions could be made in a simple majority voting process. Then, like Tullock and even though he did not refer to Kant, Buchanan distinguished behaving ethically or morally – that is being "interest[ed] in the welfare of his fellow citizen" (1961a: 340) – from utility maximization. And his conclusion was similar to Tullock's:

> as the size of the group increases, any tacit adherence to moral or ethical principles that might inhibit individual utility-maximizing behaviour becomes more difficult to secure. . . . the individual's interest in the welfare of his fellow citizen falls off sharply as the group is enlarged. (1961a: 340).

Hence, one should distinguish small groups – in which individuals cooperate – from large ones – in which individuals no longer cooperate because the ethical rule of behavior loses strength.

Size also played a role in the analysis Buchanan and Kafoglis developed in "A Note on Public Goods Supply" (1963). In their demonstration that private, cooperative, and voluntary arrangements, could be more efficient than the public provision of public goods, Buchanan and Kafoglis noted that there were circumstances in which private arrangements would be too costly to settle as "when the interactions extend over a large number of persons" (1963: 412).

It was therefore clear: for Buchanan, when the number of individuals is not too large private arrangements are possible; there is no need to rely on a centralized and coercive organization of collective action. As to why individuals cooperate in small groups, Buchanan would answer later, after having first found out the concept of club.

---

[77] The paper appears under the title "Simple Majority Voting and The Theory of Games" in *The Calculus of Consent* (1962: chapter 11, 143–164).

6.5.2 Clubs, and the Pricing of Public Goods

Buchanan started to work on clubs in 1964. He first drafted different versions of a paper that he never completed – that we treat here as a single manuscript (1964b) – before eventually writing "An Economic Theory of Clubs" (1965a). His goal was really to find out what would be the price individuals have to pay for the public goods provided in a (small) group and on how the costs of the public goods would be shared among the group members. And, since he had started to work on the question by studying the pricing of highway services, it was again the case he analyzed.

From the section on the pricing of highway services, one remembers that, in 1952, Buchanan envisaged that consumers could be charged a two-part tariff: A charge per unit of consumption, set at the level of the marginal cost, and a flat or fixed fee, to cover the costs of the provision of the good or the difference between the marginal and average cost, given that public goods and club goods are frequently decreasing cost industries. In 1964, Buchanan changed his mind and rejected the two-part tariff – which is quite ironical if one remembers that such tariff is commonly linked to a club pricing mechanism (Sandler and Tschirhart 1980: 1504). He preferred club pricing to include no charge per unit, no variable part. Buchanan even suggested that it would be better to stop talking of prices and to refer to "shares" (1965a: 12), because "[u]sers pay a share in the common costs of providing the facility" (1964b). As prices, those shares could or should differ from one individual to the other. Buchanan's assumption of "equal sharing" was made "[f]or simplicity" but was "not necessary for the analysis." (1965a: 4) The principle of individualization remained central in Buchanan's analysis. Or price discrimination (as in Wiseman 1957: 64). The difference should reflect, first, the spillover costs each individual generates in consuming the good and, second, the willingness to pay for the good. These two principles remained important.

Buchanan also changed his mind about how to take congestion into account in clubs. Club members – motorists, for instance – should no longer be asked to pay for the spillover costs and club goods should no longer be priced on the marginal social cost: [t]he club approach ... involves no attempt to impose a charge on users that reflects spillover congestion costs. (Buchanan 1964b).[78] The reason seemed to have been that the externalities generated by highway users were nonseparable and, as Davis and Whinston had demonstrated,

---

[78] He had "come to the view that all the stuff on trying to 'price' highways by measuring marginal costs of congestion, a position that [he] firmly supported in the past, is conceptually wrong because it is impossible." (Buchanan to Tolley, October 7, 1964, BP, Correspondence, 1951–2014, T (2 of 2), 1959–1970, Box: 96, Folder: 2).

marginal cost pricing could be used only when technological externalities are separable (1962: 247).[79] If the spillover costs could thus no longer be included from the cost side, they should be taken into account from the benefit side.[80] They were no longer paid by those who create the spillover effects but by those who suffer from them – if they are willing to do so – as foregone benefits. Buchanan (1964b) now claimed: "The costs of congestion enter the analysis through their effects on the estimated benefits to be received by final consumers." Each club member is characterized by a certain willingness to pay for additional members – a "rate (which may be negative) at which the individual is willing to give up (accept) money in exchange for additional members in the sharing group" (Buchanan 1965a: 4). Each additional member generates costs once in the club. Thus, "when the marginal benefits that he secures from having an additional member ... are just equal to the marginal costs that he incurs from adding a member ... an individual attains full equilibrium in club size" (1965a: 5).

Pareto optimality requires that each share is based on the individual's willingness to pay for having additional members in the club as well as the willingness to pay for the goods produced by the club. That was the second element that club pricing should include. Buchanan (1965a: 5) thus added another principle stating that, for each individual the "marginal rate of substitution between goods Xj [the club good] and Xr [the numeraire good], in consumption, must be equal to the marginal rate of substitution between these same two goods in 'production' or exchange." This was exactly the condition he had used in his 1955 comment to Samuelson. It reflected his conviction that each individual should pay the price that he or she is willing to pay. Clubs were thus meant to implement this important condition. This was also clearly a reason for which club shares would be individualized and different from one individual to the other. Again, Buchanan was implying that his condition and only his could guarantee a Pareto-optimal allocation of resources.

Thus, clubs were a means to implement the prices individuals were ready to pay. Complementarily, without clubs for public goods individuals would pay a price that does not satisfy their preferences. Clubs were also a means to avoid coercion.

---

[79] An externality is separable if the consumption or output of i does not affect the marginal utility or cost of j. Otherwise, it is non-separable.

[80] "[T]he use of price to restrict usage to some 'optimal' level of traffic remains relevant [but], we should, I now think, come at price differently, and not via the cost side at all." (Buchanan to Tolley, October 7, 1964, BP, Correspondence, 1951–2014, T (2 of 2), 1959–1970, Box: 96, Folder: 2).

6.5.3 Clubs, Small Numbers, and Property Rights

"An Economic Theory of Clubs" was published in February 1965. Immediately after, Buchanan started to write "Ethical Rules, Expected Values, and Large Numbers" (1965b), an article that Buchanan saw as a sequel to his paper on clubs. On March 15, 1965, he mentioned to McKean "a piece that I plan to send off to an ethics journal . . . it spells out the importance of small numbers."[81] Buchanan indeed detailed why individuals cooperate in certain environments and not in others.

Unsurprisingly, the choice to cooperate or not to cooperate depends on the gains, and costs, individuals expect to receive and incur from their behavior. Those gains then obviously depend on how others behave. More precisely, since no one can know in advance how others will behave, they depend on each individual's "own predictions about the behavior of others" (1965b: 3). Indeed, it is a matter of probability – "The expected values depend, of course, on the probabilities that the individual assigns to the various patterns of behavior for 'others' than himself" (5; see also 1968a: 85) These probabilities in turn depend on the impact or influence each individual believes his or her behavior will have on others. Individuals cooperate after having contemplated whether or not their behavior will "exert some influence on the behavior of others in the group" (86). However, the effect such a belief will have on cooperation can be positive or negative. An individual "may behave cooperatively hoping that his . . . 'rivals' will emulate his . . . action" (Buchanan 1967a: 121). Or, by contrast, he may decide not to cooperate since he expects that "his own action in contribution will lower, not increase, the probability of others' making contributions of their own" (Buchanan 1968a: 86).

Thus, in large groups, individuals anticipate that their behavior will not influence the behavior of others – "Only in such large groups will the individual consider his own action to exert substantially no effect on the actions of others" (1965b: 9). They consequently behave non-strategically, "react[ing] or adjust-[ing] to the behavior of 'others' in a manner similar to his reaction to natural environment" (1967b: 113). Natural means that individuals treat others as part of *nature*, taking their behavior as given and as independent of their own – "The behavior of the other is embodied as data in the choice calculus, but the other person is not considered to be subject to influence or control, positively or negatively" (111). Therefore, individuals behave as if they were independent from others. They ignore the interdependencies that link them to others. They

---

[81] Buchanan to Roland McKean, March 15, 1965, BP, "Unofficial Academic Letters," 1957–1970, Box: 102, Folder: 6.

simply maximize their own, private, utility. Or, as Buchanan put it, they follow "the private maxim" or "the expediency criterion" (1965b: 2).

Now, since the decision to maximize one's utility, to follow the expediency criterion or the private maxim comes from the belief that each individual is independent from others, one understands that each individual makes this choice by ignoring what others do. Whether or not others cooperate, each individual prefers not to cooperate – "In a group of critically large size, the individual will tend to adopt the rule of following the expediency criterion even if he thinks that *all* of his fellow citizens are saints" (1965b: 7; emphasis in original). Convinced that they are not able to influence the behavior of others, no one will change his own behavior. No reason can lead individuals to choose to behave differently – "Rationally, he cannot adopt the moral law as a principle for his own behavior" (1965b: 7). Even if they understand that defection is not the best strategy and that would be better off by cooperating with others. Buchanan was rather clear about that: "The individual in a large-group, public-goods interaction ... face[s] ... no pressure or incentive to behave cooperatively," because he behaves independently from others (1967a: 121). As a consequence, the individuals who are in large groups are trapped in what Buchanan called the "large number dilemma" (1965b), which is a form of prisoner's dilemma: "The dilemma is a real one, and it is similar to, although not identical with, that which is commonly discussed in game theory as 'the prisoners' dilemma'." (8). This situation corresponds to what Samuelson, and other economists, viewed as the standard case of market failure.

Let us note here that, to Buchanan, "[t]he individual is caught in a dilemma by the nature of his situation; he has no sensation of securing benefits at the expense of others in any personal manner" (1968a: 83). Not cooperating, following the expediency criterion, means that the individuals maximize their own utility without taking into account or acknowledging the presence of others. Each of them behaves as if others were not there. In other words, choosing not to cooperate *in a large group* was not interpreted by Buchanan as meaning that individuals would free ride. From this perspective, Buchanan found the terminology used in public economics about free riding "misleading" (1968a: 83). Indeed, free riding "suggests some deliberate effort on the part of the choosing individual to secure benefits at the expense of his fellows" (Buchanan 1965b: 9). It implies that individuals try "to shift a major share of the burden onto the other while himself securing a share of the benefits" (1967: 114). They really adopt antisocial behaviors (see Marciano 2015). Or, to use another of Buchanan's words, they try to "exploit" others. In other words, a free rider acknowledges and takes into account others, which is incompatible with how individuals are supposed to behave in large groups. Free riding is more a behavior that could arise, but don't, in small groups.

In small groups such as an "isolated setting" (Buchanan 1965b: 6) of three persons or "a desert island" (6) or when "personal interaction is recognized" (Buchanan 1968a: 86), the situation is different. Indeed, "utility maximization in a small number setting will not exhibit the observable properties of utility maximization in a large number setting" (Buchanan 1978: 366). More precisely, individuals no longer follow their "narrowly defined self-interest" (366) but rather adopt "moral or ethical principles" (Buchanan 1961a: 340). Individuals adapt their behavior to the behavior of others or, to use Buchanan's words, they behave "strategically" (1968a: 91). They no longer ignore the interdependencies that link them to others. Indeed, by contrast with what happens in a large number of environments, individuals are aware that their behavior matters and may influence others: Each individual "will tend to recognize that his own choice of a rule, and subsequent adherence to it, will to some considerable extent influence the similar choices to be made and followed by the other two members" (1965b: 6). Or, "So long as the interaction is limited to small groups, [the individual] will recognize that his own action can exert some influence on the behavior of others in the group" (1967a: 115).

In particular, an individual who "contributes nothing . . . may assess the probability of noncooperation on the part of others higher than if he contributes some share. This change alone may be sufficient, on rational grounds, to cause him to contribute" (Buchanan 1968a: 86). Individuals cooperate because they know and anticipate that this behavior will lead others to cooperate too (and that defection would probably lead them to defect too). It thus seems reasonable to claim that, to Buchanan, the individuals who are in a small group or who are not narrow utility maximizers are unconditional cooperators, as long as they are in a small group or among other ethical individuals. They have a dominant strategy that consists in cooperating with the provision of the public goods or internalize the externalities their behavior can generate. To put it differently, they act collectively. To Buchanan, there was no doubt that in small groups, the probability to follow this Kantian principle was higher than in large groups (see also 1978: 365). Therefore, the large number dilemma disappears. Individuals cooperate, contributing to the provision of public goods or internalizing the external effects of their actions on others. Free riding does not even exist.

The willingness to cooperate, as likely as it was, was not guaranteed without certain rules. Individuals could indeed behave opportunistically, "find[ing] it to [their] advantage to conceal [their] true preferences and to give false signals about those preferences to [their] opponents-partners" (Buchanan 1968b: 81). Such behaviors could be tolerated only up to a certain point (Buchanan 1968a:

357–358). They were dangerous. That some individuals could free ride was an obstacle to collective action. Individuals would indeed "be reluctant to enter voluntarily into cost-sharing arrangements ... [i]f they think that exclusion will not be fully possible, that they can expect to secure benefits as free riders without really becoming full-fledged contributing members of the club" (Buchanan 1965a: 13–14). Free riders should be excluded from the group. Exclusion – that is, the exclusion of those who do not pay the membership fees – therefore has to be possible. In small groups, where relationships were personal, "the possibility of *excluding* genuine non-conformists will normally be present" (1968b: 87). But it was much efficient if property rights were used to guarantee the exclusion of free riders, to prevent free-riding behaviors and therefore to secure the benefits of inclusion in the club to its members (1965a: 13; see also Buchanan and Tullock 1962: 44). Property rights were necessary to allow the exclusion of potential free riders.

A club was therefore viewed as an institutional arrangement including the individuals who were willing to cooperate – that is ready to adopt an ethical rule of behavior – and to exclude those who could be tempted to free ride. As Buchanan (1965a: 13) wrote, a "theory of club is ... a theory of optimal exclusion, as well as one of inclusion." As a mechanism, clubs could be used to deal with many instances of market failures. Local goods – a swimming pool, which was the example Buchanan took in his 1965 article, or a highway network as in the preliminary 1964 version – come immediately to mind. Thus, clubs seem to be rather small groups. However, there was no conceptual reason why clubs could not exist to deal with less impure and less local public goods, and even with pure public goods in the standard, Samuelsonian sense of the word – such as defense. Buchanan cited lighthouses or a vaccine as examples of goods that could be dealt with through clubs, provided that property rights were defined to prohibit free riders from benefiting of the good. Potentially, to Buchanan (1965a: 13), there was no limit to physical excludability: "Physical exclusion is possible, given sufficient flexibility in property law, in almost all imaginable cases, including those in which the interdependence lies in the act of consuming itself."

7 Conclusion

James Buchanan was a public finance economist. It is the field to which belongs his dissertation, as well as many important articles and books that he wrote over his career and he is well known for that. Buchanan's reputation also holds to his contribution to public choice, constitutional economics, and to the publication of *The Calculus of Consent* (Buchanan and Tullock 1962). This does represent two independent sets of works. Indeed, Buchanan became interested in institutions, in voting rules, and collective action *because* he was trying to deal with a problem in public finance. Put differently, Buchanan needed public choice because of his work in public finance. Public choice, at least to Buchanan, grew out of public finance. This is documented historically in this book, thus completing claims already made (see, in particular, Wagner 2017). The difference with previous work regarding this connection is that we do not insist so much on "The Pure Theory of Government Finance" (1949b) as the source, the matrix of the works Buchanan wrote subsequently. This work became important because Buchanan later developed and elaborated on the arguments he had then sketched in 1949. And he developed these arguments because of external factors that pushed him towards a theory of collective action.

What we have thus shown is that, in this process, Buchanan was mainly motivated by academic and scientific objectives – the defense of voluntary exchange theory, of Wicksell's work; the desire to answer Samuelson and to reconcile their respective works; etc. Ideology was not absent, however. We have seen how important Galbraith's book was for Buchanan, and that his opposition was also motivated by a rejection of dirigisme and the dangers of collectivizing the economy and society. But Buchanan didn't write against Galbraith just to criticize him and his theories. It was part of his general project in public finance, which he had begun with his thesis. Other contextual elements may have played a role, which we do not deny. We have left them aside because their impact on Buchanan's research program is less clear, more evasive, or more difficult to document than the impact of these academic factors (at least, with the knowledge we have and the archives available so far).

From this perspective, it seems clear that Buchanan's interest in institutions and collective action stemmed from his belief in voluntary exchange theory. This meant that taxes should be viewed as prices, and therefore that individuals bought public goods and services exactly as they bought private goods. And, as with private goods, individuals should be asked to pay a price corresponding to the marginal utility they get from consuming the good or service in question. That was quite a strong claim to make. The Italian public finance theorists, who had inspired Buchanan, had rejected it rather early on. And the only Anglo-Saxon economist familiar with voluntary exchange, Musgrave, rejected the possibility that the relationship between taxpayers and the government could take the form of an exchange. And yet, Buchanan stuck to it. Even though it turned out that the theory was extremely difficult to implement – no one really believed it could be – Buchanan stuck to it. And asked how would it be possible to price public goods when one cannot rely on the market? Which nonmarket mechanism could be used that would mimic the market, to implement individualized prices and enable individuals to pay for what they consume.

In fact, Buchanan could not abandon the pricing of public goods because it was more than a technical hypothesis about resource allocation. It was a fundamental principle underpinning his conception of social order. Put another way, the story we have told tells us at least as much about Buchanan's social philosophy as it does about his tax philosophy and economic theory. Buchanan believed in voluntary exchange because it's a theory based on the premise that everyone gets what he buys (and is willing to pay for it). And he believed in this theory because it rests on willingness, the individual desire to pay for the public goods consumed and the external effects caused. Then, when he began to take an interest in nonmarket mechanisms, he naturally retained the same principle: Individuals can be trusted to organize their interactions, to cooperate and devise arrangements for managing public goods or eliminating the external effects that affect their actions, just as they can be trusted to pay for the public goods and services they consume. This belief, this conviction, is crucial to understanding Buchanan's approach to public finance, that is, Buchanan's public economics, but also his interest in collective action. It is one of the main subsidiary claims of this book.

Admittedly, by the early 1970s, a certain form of pessimism had taken hold of Buchanan, as can be seen in *The Limits of Liberty* (1975a) or "The Samaritan's Dilemma" (1975b). However, we suggest that these works should be read in the continuity and perspective of what Buchanan had written before, more than as inaugurating a new period in his career. Buchanan still believed in the idea that individuals were ready to cooperate in principle, that is. In practice, the realm of private, voluntary, and collective action had narrowed. Hence the need to rely more on a social contract.

References

BP (Buchanan Papers): James M. Buchanan papers, C0246. George Mason University. Libraries. Special Collections Research Center.

Arrow, Kenneth J. 1951. *Social Choice and Individual Values*. New York: Wiley.

Bator, Francis M. 1958. "The Anatomy of Market Failure," *Quarterly Journal of Economics* 72 (3): 351–379.

1960. *The Question of Government Spending. Public Needs and Private Wants*. New York: Harper & Brothers.

Benham Frederic, C. 1934a. "Review *Principii di Economia Finanziaria* by A. De Viti de Marco; *Grundlehren der Finanzwirtschaft* by A. De Viti de Marco," *Economica* 1 (3): 364–367.

1934b. "Notes on the Pure Theory of Public Finance," *Economica* 1 (4): 436–458.

1938. *Economics a General Textbook for Students*. London: Pitman and Sons.

Boettke, Peter J. 2023. "Dishwater of the Orthodoxy," in Carroll Ríos de Rodríguez and Andrés Marroquín (eds.), *A Companion to James Buchanan*. Guatemala: Universidad Francisco Marroquín, 279–289.

2019. "The Allure and Tragedy of Ideological Blinders Left, Right, and Center: A Review Essay of Nancy Maclean's *Democracy in Chains*," *Research in the History of Economic Thought and Methodology* 37B: 123–147.

2020. *The Soul of Classical Political Economy. James M. Buchanan from the Archives*. Mercatus Center: George Mason University.

and Alain Marciano. 2015. "The Past, Present and Future of Virginia Political Economy," *Public Choice* 163: 53–65.

and John Kroencke. 2020. "The Real Purpose of the Program: A Case Study in James M. Buchanan's Efforts at Academic Entrepreneurship to "Save the Books" in economics," *Public Choice* 183: 227–245.

J. R. Clark and John Kroencke. 2020. "Academic Entrepreneurship in Sometimes Hostile Environments. James Buchanan and the Virginia School of Political Economy," *The Independent Review* 27 (1): 121–140.

Boulding, Kenneth E. 1959. "Review of *The Affluent Society* by John Kenneth Galbraith," *Review of Economics and Statistics* 41 (1): 81.

Brownlee, Oscar H. 1961. "User Prices versus Taxes." in James M. Buchanan (ed.), *Public Finances: Needs, Sources, and Utilization*, National Bureau of Economic Research, Princeton: Princeton University Press, 421–432.

and Walter W. Heller. 1956. "Highway Development and Financing," *American Economic Review* 46 (2): 232–250.

Buchanan, James M. 1947. "A Theory of Financial Balance in a Federal State," Mimeo. BP, Term Project for Economics 362, March 5, Box: 16, Folder: 1.

1948. "The Problem of Fiscal Inequality in a Federal State," mimeo. BP.

1949a. "The Pure Theory of Government Finance: A Suggested Framework," mimeo, BP, "The Pure Theory of Government Finance: A Suggested Approach" drafts and correspondence, Box: 196, Folder: 8.

1949b. "The Pure Theory of Government Finance: A Suggested Approach," *Journal of Political Economy* 57 (6): 496–505.

1950. "Federalism and Fiscal Equity," *American Economic Review* 40 (4): 583–599.

1951. "Knut Wicksell on Marginal Cost Pricing," *Southern Economic Journal* 18 (2): 173–178.

1952a. "The Pricing of Highway Services," *National Tax Journal* 5: 97–106.

1952b. "Wicksell on Fiscal Reform, A Comment," *American Economic Review* 42: 599–602.

1953. "The Politics of Economic Policy," mimeo, BP, Box: 186, Folder: 10.

1954a. "Resource Allocation and the Highway System," mimeo, BP.

1954b. "Consumption Interdependence and the Interpretation of Social Cost," mimeo, BP.

1954c. "Social Choice, Democracy, and Free Markets," *Journal of Political Economy* 62 (2): 114–123.

1954d. "Individual Choice in Voting and the Market," *Journal of Political Economy* 62 (4): 334–343.

1954(e1–e4). "Private Ownership and Common Usage: The Road Case Re-Examined." mimeo, BP.

1955a. "A Note of the Pure Theory of Public Expenditure," mimeo, BP, "A Note on the Pure Theory of Public Expenditure" drafts and correspondence with Samuelson, 1955, Box: 176, Folder: 9.

1955b. "Painless Pavements: Highways by High Finance." mimeo, BP, "Painless Pavements: Highways by High Finance", February 9, Box: 182, Folder: 5.

1955c. *Traffic, Tolls and Taxes: The Economics of the Nation's Highway Problem.* mimeo, BP, Box: 216, Folder: 10–11–12.

1956a. "Private Ownership and Common Usage: The Road Case ReExamined," *Southern Economic Journal* 22 (3): 305–316.

1956b. "Notes on Samuelson's Theory of Public Expenditure," mimeo, BP, "A Note on the Pure Theory of Public Expenditure" drafts and correspondence with Samuelson, 1955, Box: 176, Folder: 9.

1957. "Federal Expenditure and State Functions," in *Federal Expenditure Policy for Economic Growth and Stability*. Washington, DC: Joint Economic Committee, 174–179.

1958a. "Ceteris Paribus: Some Notes on Methodology", *Southern Economic Journal* 24 (3): 259–270.

1958b. "Ignorance, Ethics and Political Economy," mimeo BP, in "Positive Economics, Welfare Economics, and Political Economy" drafts, notes, and correspondence, 1958, Box: 187, Folder: 2.

1958c. "The Thomas Jefferson Center for Studies in Political Economy," *The University of Virginia News Letter* 35 (2): 5–8.

1958d. "Preliminary Statement of Ford Application," mimeo, BP.

1958e. *Public Principles of Public Debt: A Defense and Restatement*, Homewood: R. D. Irwin.

1958f. "Statement", in Federal Expenditure Policy for Economic Growth and Stability, Hearings before the Subcommittee on Fiscal Policy of the Joint Economic Committee, Congress of the United States, United States Government Printing Office, Washington, 77–79.

1959. "Positive Economics, Welfare Economics, and Political Economy," *Journal of Law and Economics* 2 (October): 124–138.

1960a. "Review: *The Theory of Public Finance: A Study in Public Economy* by Richard A. Musgrave," *Southern Economic Journal* 26 (3): 234–238.

1960b. "La scienza delle finanze. The Italian Tradition in Fiscal Theory," in James M. Buchanan, *Fiscal Theory and Political Economy*. Chapel Hill: University of North Carolina Press, pp. 24–74.

1960c. Thomas Jefferson Center Annual Report, mimeo, BP, Box 383, Folder 13.

1960d. *The Public Finances. An Introductory Textbook*. Homewood, IL: R. D. Irwin.

1961a. "Simple Majority Voting, Game Theory and Resource Use," *Canadian Journal of Economics and Political Science* 27 (3): 337–348.

1961b. "Comments." in James Buchanan (ed.), *Public Finances: Needs, Sources, and Utilization*, Princeton: Princeton University Press, 122–129.

1962a. "Politics, Policy and the Pigovian Margins," *Economica* 29 (113): 17–28.

1962b. "The American Revolution and the Modern Economy," mimeo, BP, "The American Revolution and the Modern Economy" edited typescripts, 1962, Box: 117.

1963. "The Free Society: Fact, Faith, of Fiction," mimeo, BP, Box: 153, Folder: 4.

1964a. "The 'Club' Approach to Highways," mimeo, BP, "An Economic Theory of Clubs", 1965, Box: 141, Folder: 10.

1964b. "What Should Economists Do?" *Southern Economic Journal* 30: 213–222.

1965a. "An Economic Theory of Clubs," *Economica* 32 (125): 1–14.

1965b. "Ethical Rules, Expected Values, and Large Numbers," *Ethics* 76 (1): 1–13.

1966. "Externality in Tax Response," *Southern Economic Journal* 33 (1): 35–42.

1967a. "Cooperation and Conflict in Public Goods Interactions," *Economic Inquiry* 5 (2): 109–121.

1967b. *Public Finance in Democratic Process: Fiscal Institutions and Individual Choice.* Indianapolis: Liberty Press.

1968a. *The Demand and Supply of Public Goods.* Liberty Fund (1999).

1968b. "A Behavioral Theory of Pollution," *Economic Inquiry* 6 (5): 347–358.

1969. *Cost and Choice: An Inquiry in Economic Theory.* Chicago: Markham.

1975a. *The Limits of Liberty. Between Anarchy and Leviathan.* Chicago: Chicago University Press.

1975b. "The Samaritan's Dilemma," in Edmund S. Phelps (ed.), *Altruism, Morality and Economic Theory,* New York: Sage Foundation, 71–85.

1978. "Markets, States, and the Extent of Morals," *American Economic Review* 68 (2): 364–368.

1987. "The Constitution of Economic Policy," *American Economic Review* 77 (3): 243–250.

1995. "Interview," *The Region,* September, www.minneapolisfed.org/article/1995/interview-with-james-buchanan.

1998. "Majoritarian Logic," *Public Choice* 97: 13–21.

2007A. *Economics from the Outside In: "Better Than Plowing" and Beyond.* College Station: Texas A&M University Press.

and Charles Goetz. 1972. "Efficiency Limits of Fiscal Mobility: An Assessment of the Tiebout Model," *Journal of Public Economics* 1: 25–43.

and Gordon Tullock. 1962. *The Calculus of Consent: Logical Foundations of Constitutional Democracy.* Ann Arbor: University of Michigan Press.

and Milton Z. Kafoglis. 1963. "A Note on Public Goods Supply," *American Economic Review* 53 (3): 403–414.

and W. Craig Stubblebine. 1962. "Externality," *Economica* 29 (116): 371–384.

Coase, Ronald H. 1959. "The Federal Communication Commission," *Journal of Law and Economics* 2: 1–40.

1960. "The Problem of Social Cost," *Journal of Law and Economics* 3 (October): 1–44.

1993. "Law and Economics at Chicago." *Journal of Law and Economics* 36(1), 239–254.

Davis, Otto A. and Andrew Whinston. 1962. "Externalities, Welfare, and the Theory of Games," *Journal of Political Economy* 70 (3): 241–262.

Desmarais-Tremblay, Maxime. 2016. *La théorisation des dépenses publiques de Richard A. Musgrave: Essai d'histoire de la pensée et d'épistémologie économiques*. Université Paris 1 Panthéon-Sorbonne; Université de Lausanne, https://hal.archives-ouvertes.fr/tel-01475790.

Einaudi, Luigi. 1929. *Contributo all ricerca della 'ottima imposta'*. Università Bocconi Editrice: Milano.

Enke, Stephen. 1955. "More on the Misuse of Mathematics in Economics: A Rejoinder," *Review of Economics and Statistics* 37 (2): 131–133.

Fischel, William A. 2000. "Municipal Corporations, Homeowners, and the Benefit View of the Property Tax," mimeo, Dartmouth College.

Fleury Jean-Baptiste and Alain Marciano. 2018a. "The making of a constitutionalist: James Buchanan on education," *History of Political Economy* 50 (3): 511–548.

2018b. "The Sound of Silence: A Review Essay of Nancy MacLean's *Democracy in Chains: The Deep History of the Radical Right's Stealth Plan for America*," *Journal of Economic Literature* 56 (4): 1492–1537.

Galbraith, John K. 1949. "The American Economy: Substance and Myth," in John W. Chase (ed.), *Years of the Modern: An American Appraisal*, New York: Longmans, Green, 151–174.

1958. *The Affluent Society*. Boston: Houghton Mifflin.

2001. *"The Essential Galbraith,"* essays selected and edited by Andrea D. Williams, New York: Houghton Migglin Company.

Hansjürgens, Bernd. 2000. "The Influence of Knut Wicksell on Richard Musgrave and James Buchanan," *Public Choice* 103 (1–2): 95–116.

Heilbroner, Robert. 1989. "Rereading *The Affluent Society*," *Journal of Economic Issues* 23 (2): 367–377.

Hitch, Charles J. and Roland N. McKean. 1961. "What Can Managerial Economics Contribute to Economic Theory?" *American Economic Review* 51 (2): 147–154.

Hotelling, Harold. 1938. "The General Welfare in Relation to Problems of Taxation and of Railway and Utility Rates," *Econometrica* 6 (3): 242–269.

Hutt, William H. 1936. *Economists and the Public: A Study of Competition and Opinion*. London: Cape.

1940. "The Concept of Consumers' Sovereignty," *The Economic Journal* 50(197), 66–77.

Jewkes, John and Sylvia Jewkes. 1961. *The Genesis of the British National Health Service*. Oxford: Blackwell.

Johnson, Marianne. 2005. "Wicksell's Unaminity Rule Buchanan's Dominance Considered," *American Journal of Economics and Sociology* 64 (4): 1049–1071.

2010. "Wicksell's Social Philosophy and His Unanimity Rule," *Review of Social Economy* 68 (2): 187–204.

2015. "Public Goods, Market Failure, and Voluntary Exchange," in Alain Marciano and Steven G. Medema (eds.), *Market Failure in Context, History of Political Economy* 47 (suppl. 1). Durham, NC: Duke University Press, 174–198.

Joint Committee on the Economic Report. 1950. "Highways and the nation's economy, united states, government printing office, Washington." www .jec.senate.gov/reports/81st congress/highways and the nation's economy (31).pdf.

Knight, Frank. 1924. "Some Fallacies in the Interpretation of Social Cost," *Quarterly Journal of Economics* 38 (4): 582–606.

Lerner, Abba P. 1944. *The Economics of Control*. New-York: Macmillan.

Levy, David and Sandra Peart. 2020. *Towards an Economics of Natural Equals: A Documentary History of the Early Virginia School*. Cambridge: Cambridge University Press.

MacLean, Nancy. 2017. *Democracy in Chains: The Deep History of the Radical Right's Stealth Plan for America*. New York: Penguin Books.

Marciano, Alain. 2013. "Why Market Failures Are Not a Problem: James Buchanan on Market Imperfections, Voluntary Cooperation, and Externalities." *History of Political Economy* 45(2): 223–254.

2015. "Buchanan on Pro-social Behaviors: Why Is Ethics Necessary," *Œconomia* 5 (3): 295–311.

2016. "Buchanan's Non-coercive Economics for Self-interested Individuals: Ethics, Small Groups and the Social Contract," *Journal of the History of Economic Thought* 38 (1): 1–20.

2018 "From Highway to Clubs: Buchanan and the Pricing of Public Goods", in Richard E. Wagner (ed.), *James M. Buchanan: A Theorist of Political Economy and Social Philosophy*, Cham: Palgrave-Macmillan, 713–737.

2019a. "Buchanan and Public Finance: The Tennessee Years." *Review of Austrian Economics* 32, 21–46.

2020. "How Buchanan's Concern for the South Shaped His First Academic Works," *Public Choice* 183: 247–271.

2021. "Retrospectives: James Buchanan: Clubs and Alternative Welfare Economics." *Journal of Economic Perspectives* 35 (3): 243–256.

Marciano, Alain and Steve Medema. 2015. "Introduction," in Alain Marciano and Steven G. Medema (eds.), *Market Failure in Context, History of Political Economy* 47 (Suppl. 1). Durham, NC: Duke University Press, 1–19.

Margolis, Julius. 1955. "A Comment on the Pure Theory of Public Expenditure," *Review of Economics and Statistics* 37 (4): 347–349.

1957. "Welfare Criteria, Pricing and Decentralization of a Public Service," *Quarterly Journal of Economics* 71 (3): 448–463.

Meade, James E. 1952. "External Economies and Diseconomies in a Competitive Situation," *Economic Journal*, 62 (245): 54–67.

1963. "Review of the Calculus of Consent: Logical Foundations of Constitutional Democracy," *Economic Journal* 73 (289): 101–104.

Medema, Steven G. 2009. *The Hesitant Hand: Taming Self-Interest in the History of Economics Ideas*. Princeton: Princeton University Press.

2020. "Exceptional and Unimportant"? Externalities, Competitive Equilibrium, and the Myth of a Pigovian Tradition," *History of Political Economy* 52 (1): 135–170.

Musgrave, Richard A. 1939. "The Voluntary Exchange Theory of Public Economy," *Quarterly Journal of Economics* 53 (2): 213–237.

1941. "The Planning Approach in Public Economy: A Reply," *Quarterly Journal of Economics* 55 (2): 319–324.

1959. *The Theory of Public Finance*. New York: McGraw Hill.

Netzer, D. 1952. "Toll Roads and the crisis in highway finance." *National Tax Journal* 5(2), 107–119.

Owen, Wilfred and Charles L. Dearing. 1951. *Toll Roads and the Problem of Highway Modernization*. Washington (DC): Brookings Institution..

Peacock, Alan T. 1961. *The Welfare Society*. Unservile State Papers, n° 2, p. 21.

Pigou, Arthr C. 1920. *The Economics of Wealth and Welfare*. London: Macmillan.

1920. *The Economics of Welfare*. London: MacMillan.

Redfield, Charles E. and Edward A. Lutz. (1952) "Review of Get the Folks Out of the Mud!" *Public Administration Review* 12(2): 126–131.

Rothbard, Murray. 1956. "Toward a Reconstruction of Utility and Welfare Economics." https://mises.org/rothbard/toward.pdf. Accessed October 3, 2015.

Ruggles, Nancy. 1949b. "Recent Developments in the Theory of Marginal Cost Pricing," *Review of Economic Studies* 17(2): 107–126.

1949a. "The Welfare Basis of the Marginal Cost Pricing," *Review of Economic Studies* 17 (1): 29–46.

Samuelson, Paul A. 1954. "The Pure Theory of Public Expenditure," *Review of Economics and Statistics* 36 (4): 387–389.

1955. "Diagrammatic Exposition of a Theory of Public Expenditure," *Review of Economics and Statistics* 37 (4): 350–356.

Samuelson, Paul A. 1958. "Aspects of Public Expenditure," *Review of Economics and Statistics* 40 (4): 332–338.

Sandler, Todd and John T. Tschirhart. 1980. "The Economic Theory of Clubs: An Evaluative Survey," *Journal of Economic Literature* 18 (4): 1481–1521.

Scitovsky, Tibor. 1954. "Two Concepts of External Economies," *Journal of Political Economy* 62 (2): 143–151.

Simons, Henry C. 1937. "Review of the First Principles of Public Finance, by Antonio de Viti de Marco," *American Economic Review* 45 (October): 712–717.

Stanfield, J. R. 1983. "'The Affluent Society' after Twenty-Five Years," *Journal of Economic Issues* 17 (3): 589–607.

Sternsher, Bernard. 1962. "Liberalism in the Fifties: The Travail of Redefinition," *The Antioch Review* 22 (3): 315–331.

Tiebout, Charles. M. 1956. "A Pure Theory of Local Expenditures," *Journal of Political Economy* 64 (5): 416–424.

1961. "An Economic Theory of Fiscal Decentralization," in James Buchanan (ed.), *Public Finances: Needs, Sources, and Utilization*, Princeton, NJ: Princeton, 79–96.

Tullock, Gordon. 1959a. "Democratic Marginalism," Gordon Tullock papers, Box: 42, Folder: 3, Hoover Institution Archives.

1959b. "Problems of Majority Voting," *Journal of Political Economy* 67 (6): 571–579.

Wagner, Richard E. 2017. *James M. Buchanan and Liberal Political Economy.* Lanham, MD: Lexington Books.

Weingroff, Richard F. 1996, "Federal-Aid Highway Act of 1956, Creating the Interstate System," *Public Roads*, 60 (1), https://highways.dot.gov/public-roads/summer-1996/federal-aid-highway-act-1956-creating-interstate-system

Wicksell, Knut. [1896] 1958. "A New Principle of Just Taxation," translated by James M. Buchanan, in Richard A. Musgrave and Alan T. Peacock (eds.), *Classics in the Theory of Public Finance*, London: Macmillan, 72–118.

1896. *Finanztheoretische Untersuchungen.* Jena: Gustav Fischer.

1934. *Lectures on Political Economy.* New York: Macmillan.

Wiseman, Jack. 1957. "The Theory of Public Utility Price-An Empty Box," *Oxford Economic Papers* 9 (1): 56–74.

Acknowledgments

The book was completed while I was in delegation at THEMA CY Cergy Paris Université UMR CNRS 8184, Cergy, France. A first version of this book was presented at a Workshop in Philosophy, Politics & Economics, The F. A. Hayek Program for Advanced Study in Philosophy, Politics, and Economics at the Mercatus Center; and at a seminar on "Liberalism and Conservatism at a Crossroads" (AGORA-CY Cergy Paris Université). I thank the participants for their comments, questions, and remarks. Many thanks to those who have read the previous versions of this manuscript. In particular Peter Boettke (also for his encouragement), Rosolino Candela, Chris Coyne, Erwin Dekker, Andrew Farrant, Yann Giraud, Catherine Marshall, John Meadowcroft, and Mikayla Novak. Many thanks to Jessica Carges, Kurtis Hingl, and Janna Lu for their invaluable help.

I would also thank the publishers who authorized me to use parts of the following articles:

Cambridge Elements ≡

Austrian Economics

Peter Boettke

George Mason University

Peter Boettke is a Professor of Economics & Philosophy at George Mason University, the BB&T Professor for the Study of Capitalism, and the director of the F. A. Hayek Program for Advanced Study in Philosophy, Politics and Economics at the Mercatus Center at George Mason University.

About the Series

This series will primarily be focused on contemporary developments in the Austrian School of Economics and its relevance to the methodological and analytical debates at the frontier of social science and humanities research, and the continuing relevance of the Austrian School of Economics for the practical affairs of public policy throughout the world.

Cambridge Elements $\equiv$

Austrian Economics

Elements in the Series

A full series listing is available at: www.cambridge.org/EAEC

Printed in the United States
by Baker & Taylor Publisher Services